THE GREATEST
ST🔑RY
NEVER TOLD

Praise for *The Greatest Story Never Told*

"The challenge of contemporary Methodism is to see cacophony morphed into symphony, to see ecclesiastical culture 'Jesus Christ-ed'" (*from the book*). Len Sweet is of the tribe of Issachar: "They knew the times and knew what to do" (1 Chron. 12:32). With brilliance of mind, Len uses words to paint pictures like an artist dabbing from a palette of many colors. He experienced Wesleyanism in his soul from his mother's singing and preaching before he knew the fire of the Spirit lit by the lamp of learning. In this book we feel our heart "newly warmed" as he takes our own ship of state from his safe harbor back to where Jesus "pilots us over tempestuous seas." We cannot take passage in these pages without saying, "Thank God, I'm a Methodist."

—Donald Haynes, pastor/professor/author/columnist for the *United Methodist Reporter*

This is a book for anyone who cares deeply about church and culture, and even more so about how we present and represent Christ in both. Sweet's message is to reclaim the passion and Spirit that set hearts ablaze for reaching the lost. I've never heard Len sing, but he hits the high notes strong and clear on this timely message to a church that needs to find its voice and sing for all it's worth! A powerful call for the church to *wake up!*

—Donald D. Cady, General Publisher, Wesleyan Publishing House, Indianapolis, Indiana

Some stories are so beautiful that art and music are the only means worthy to communicate them. Dr. Sweet is a product of just such a story, and with this book he reintroduces the tune and gets our toes tapping. Maybe we can recover our song and dance!

—Jon Middendorf, Pastor, Oklahoma City First Church of the Nazarene

LEONARD SWEET

THE GREATEST STORY NEVER TOLD

Revive Us Again

ABINGDON PRESS
Nashville

THE GREATEST STORY NEVER TOLD
REVIVE US AGAIN

Library of Congress Cataloging-in-Publication Data

Sweet, Leonard I.
  The greatest story never told : revive us again / Leonard Sweet.
    p. cm.
  ISBN 978-1-4267-4032-9 (pbk. : alk. paper) 1. Methodist Church. I. Title.
  BX8331.3.S94 2012
  287—dc23

2012008239

12 13 14 15 16 17 18 19 20 21—10 9 8 7 6 5 4 3 2 1

MANUFACTURED IN THE UNITED STATES OF AMERICA

To Brett Blair

John Wesley Redivivus

CONTENTS

Acknowledgments ix

Introduction: The Song of the "People Called Methodist" . . . xiii
"This Is My Story, This Is My Song":
God's Song in the Voices of Methodists

Chapter One: The Song of Water 1
"Lift Up Your Voice with Strength":
Holiness and Practice

Chapter Two: The Song of Fire 55
"Hearts Strangely Warmed":
The Power of Passion

Chapter Three: The Song of Wind 75
"Life in the Spirit":
The Power of Connection

Chapter Four: The Song of Earth 89
"The World Is My Parish":
The Method of Methodism as a Harmonics of Hope

Interactives 119

Notes 125

ACKNOWLEDGMENTS

I had just finished a lecture on the doctrine of holiness in the Wesleyan tradition. A prominent pastor in the audience came up to me and said: "Sweet, do you really believe that stuff?"

"Yes, I really do."

"Then for God's sake, don't repeat it," he advised as he bolted for the door.

Now I've gone and done it. I've more than repeated it. I've printed it. That means I've bolted the door behind me.

Actually, I hope this book is more of an open door, a doorway to the future that believes what John wrote from the filth and stench of the death camp of the first century, an island prison on Patmos: "Look, I have set before you an open door" (Revelation 3:8).

There are certain people who have given me the courage to open this door. First and foremost is Abingdon editor Kathy Armistead, who believed in this book even when I didn't. My agent Mark Sweeney made sure I opened a door and not a can of worms or a Pandora's box.

Buddy Marston and Gaye Marston, partners in Ludens Dei, are showing me how to be a better doorman as we struggle together to find new ways of standing at the door and ushering people into new conversations about a renaissance (re-nascence or "re-birth") in our Wesleyan tribe. Throw tribalism out the door, and it flies back in through the window. Being part of a tribe is part of our human makeup, and part of what makes us human.

Don Haynes is one of my favorite people in the world. Better than most in our tribe, Don intuits the difference between the UMC, inc. (body of Christ incarnate), and the UMC, corp. (body of Christ incorporated). The UMC, corp., is a corporate entity run according to business principles and the Order of St. Roberts (*Roberts Rules of Order*). The UMC, inc., is an incarnational body that "runs" according to the mind of Christ and St. Paul's Rules of the Spirit. His writings, musings, and notes have clarified for me how UMC, corp., turns its clergy into dependants or drudges, while UMC, inc., turns its clergy into a myriad of disciple-making life-forms. Labels slam more doors than they open. Lynn Caterson reminds me of this at the same time she is the epitome of what it means to be UMC, inc.

Kathryn Riley Ambler, a colleague in the West Virginia Annual Conference, sent me links that enabled me to eavesdrop at the thresholds of different disciplines and online trends. Unlike what Bob Dole used to say about the vice presidency—it's indoor work with no heavy lifting—there was a lot of biblical and bibliographical heavy lifting in writing this book (not to mention untold hours spent writing indoors in airplane seats). I couldn't have handled the weight without two intellectual and theological heavyweights—Betty O'Brien and Lori Wagner. Betty kept my memory grounded in the documents, while Lori kept me from sinking without a trace beneath the weight of historical convention. Every time one of Kathi's or Betty's or Lori's e-mails darkened my door, it lit up my life.

The image I chose for my role in writing this book is that of a knot of nerves that tells you about the illness of the organism. My patron saint throughout this book has been Hosea, who also experienced many hard knocks and knots. He had much to grieve about and wrote that his pillow was wet with tears. But in spite of the tears, he could say, "I will . . . make the Valley of [Trouble] a door of hope" (Hosea 2:15).

A spirit of hope and a door to the future is what I pray you take away from this book. May our theme song together be the old camp-meeting song written by W. P. MacKay:

Revive us again; fill each heart with Thy love;
May each soul be rekindled with fire from above.
Hallelujah! Thine the glory, Hallelujah! Amen.
Hallelujah! Thine the glory, revive us again.

Leonard Sweet
Rome, Italy
12 January 2012

THE SONG OF THE "PEOPLE CALLED METHODIST"

"This Is My Story, This Is My Song":
God's Song in the Voices of Methodists

> *I continue to dream and pray about a revival of holiness in*
> *our day that moves forth in mission and creates authentic*
> *community in which each person can be unleashed through the*
> *empowerment of the Spirit to fulfill God's creational intentions.*
> *— John Wesley[1]*

The shadows are lengthening over Methodism. The sound of bells tolling for the Wesleyan tribe is getting louder. The church is in the middle of an exodus, and not the biblical kind.

Really?

This book puts a question mark over the gloomiest, exclamation-point predictions of physical decline and spiritual depletion. It is not an easy assignment replacing exclamation points with question marks, especially when the dominant literature of the past two decades has been either what I call the cult of leadership or the cult of decline. In fact, one has fed off the other until sometimes you can't tell the two apart. But whether singly or together, both have been busy beavers whittling exclamation marks into deadly little daggers of condemnation and despair.

You can hear the drumroll of despair throughout Western culture. Western dominance is on the decline, as the Chinafication of the planet headlines the rise of the Wild, Wild East. The male of the species is in terminal decline, with sperm counts plummeting and the male role in the propagation of the species more and more marginal.[2] The family is in terminal decline, with American households shrinking from an average of 5.8 members in 1790 to the current level of 2.6.[3] And that's just a smattering of samples on a slippery slope downward.

But perhaps the two most talked about declines are of institutions that were founded at the same time: the "denomination," the formulation of which came out of the Westminster Assembly of Divines (1643–49); and the "nation-state," the concept of which came out of the Treaty of Westphalia (1648).

So doth [the parson] assure himself that God in all
ages hath had His servants, to whom He hath revealed
His truth, as well as to him; and that as one countrey doth
not bear all things that there may be a commerce, so neither
hath God opened, or will open, all to one, that there may be a
traffick in knowledge between the servants of God,
for the planting both of love and humility.
—*Seventeenth-century Welsh poet/priest George Herbert*[4]

Every street barker is bursting to tell you that the nation-state is either over or out-of-date and the "market state" and "micronation" is in ascendance.[5] The nation-state emerged precisely because it was better than princely states, virtual states, "state-nations," clans, feudal seigneurs, kingdoms, and townships at protecting us against all enemies; that assumption went up in the cloud of asbestos smoke that rose above the World Trade Center on September 11, 2001. The devolution revolution, which is causing trouble for all the world's nation-states, is living proof that meaning and purpose no longer come from identification with a national entity. Nationalism is in terminal decline in its ability to define the economic, cultural, or even linguistic life of the people it governs.

Likewise, it is hard to find the noun *denomination* used without the preceding adjective *declining*. The first words by one Gen-X author in an essay on hope for Methodism are these: "We are dying."[6] The accelerating state of Protestantism's eclipse has generated a cottage industry of research into why denominations are dodo birds and why people would move their memberships from the Baptist graveyard to the Methodist mausoleum. However, studies do not trace decline to "migrant worshipers." Rather, the chief cause is seen in the declining number of adults who identify with organized religion, and the failure of the children of Protestants to remain in any tradition at all.

Let us fear therefore, that we may not fear.
—Saint Augustine[7]

Suicide is the ultimate failure of imagination. Of all the denominations, The United Methodist Church is the one exhibited in a glass case as the "suicide denomination," the one that seems either to have a death wish or that continues on a course that everyone knows will one day tailspin into a death spiral. In 1870, more than 40 percent of the population of the U.S. identified themselves as Methodist. Today that figure is a little more than 5 percent. It is not without reason that for some, Methodism is like the theater critic Robert Benchley, who, when asked if he knew that heavy drinking led to a slow death, took another sip and replied, "So who's in a hurry?"[8]

I don't believe any of it. I believe God's clock keeps perfect time. I believe God may have raised up John Wesley as much for the twenty-first century as for the eighteenth century. I believe we boast a better future than the bleak catchphrase "So it goes." I believe the best days for our tribe and for the whole Wesleyan movement lie in the future. I believe Jesus can turn the water of dull, ceremonial religion into the sparkling wine of vibrant, vibrating faith. I believe that even though what we now call Methodism is in too many ways what Wesley came to get rid of, it need not come to this. Sometimes our solutions lie as much in the past as in the present or the future.

> *Instructive sound! I'm now convinced by thee,*
> *Time in its womb may bear infinity. . . .*
> —*"Upon Listening to the Vibrations of a Clock,"*
> *poem by Wesley friend John Gambold*[9]

I believe what historians call the "Methodist Revolution" is an unfinished revolution. I believe of the Methodist Revolution what the first premier of the People's Republic of China, Zhou Enlai (1898–1976), is supposed to have said when asked, "What do you think of the French Revolution?"

"It's too soon to tell."[10]

By Methodist Revolution, I am clearly distinguishing between Methodism and The United Methodist Church. Even though I am a member of the latter, I have written this book for the former as well. Methodism encompasses a diverse spectrum of movements (charismatic, pentecostal, holiness, evangelical, Arminian) and voices (Free Methodist, Nazarene, Church of God, Anglican, Wesleyan, AME, AME-Zion,

CME, CMA, Salvation Army, and so on). Would Wesley belong to any of these? What Voltaire once said of the Holy Roman Empire—it was neither holy, nor Roman, nor an empire—might arguably be said of the UMC: it is not United, not Methodist, and less a church than a bureaucracy, and sometimes less a bureaucracy than a circus. Didn't P. T. Barnum once call California a circus without a tent?

Can you imagine Wesley looking for assistants who could manage denominational decline or maintain the status quo?[11] Those very concepts would have no meaning within Methodism. Nor would the concept of a church that pays little heed to ancestral voices. That would have been unthinkable to Wesley.

If I weren't a Methodist, I'd be either a Lutheran or a Quaker. I admire both greatly—the gentle, quiet Quakers; the gutsy, gusty Lutherans. But while I admire them both, I can't deny my heritage. It is profoundly human to want to belong and be bound together in something like a "hive" or a "tribe." And my tribe is "the people called Methodist." I love my tribe, and I love the Wesleyan Way. I believe almost all roads worth taking in the last two hundred years led back to Wesley. I believe they still do. I believe in the future vibrancy of the various tribes of Wesley. That's why John Wesley is one of my compass points. There is north (the North Star is Jesus the Christ), south (Saint Augustine), east (Saint Symeon), and west (John Wesley).

People will not look forward to posterity who never look
backward to their ancestors.
—Edmund Burke (1729–97)[12]

So what's the problem?

Hello, Methodism! Methodism needs to be introduced to its true self. We've been more caught up in the drama of self-narration than the transmission of gospel-narration. Methodism has lost its true representation. Besides, when you are subjected to revisions of identity every four years, you end up either losing your identity or becoming schizophrenic.

We aren't singing our song. We aren't living our own story. We are ordered into being by the Spirit. But we are held together by how we hear ourselves, by our songs, and by how we see ourselves, by our stories.

Our situation today is much like the situations the early Methodists faced almost every day of Wesley's ministry, and the way they dealt with these situations points the way forward. One day, when Wesley was preaching, two young ruffians brought a stash of rocks to break up the meeting. But the more Wesley talked about the power of Christ to change human lives, the more they listened until one of them turned to his partner in crime, the stones dropping from his hand, and said: "He ain't a man; he ain't a man." When the sermon was over and Wesley left the platform, one of the ruffians reached out to touch the preacher's coat. Wesley stopped, put his hand on the lad's shoulder, and said, "God bless you, boy." The other vandal said to his mate with a sense of wonder: "He is a man. He is a man. He is a man of God."

This one story may have the burnish of legend about it, but the evidence abounds of John Wesley and his early Methodist preachers daily facing all sorts of rowdy crowds, mockers, and troublemakers.

It's time to recapture the Wesleyan spirit and do for our day what Wesley did for his: proclaim the gospel with confidence and power, and bless the naysayers, detractors, Christophobics, ABC-ers (Anything But Christianity people), and all whose trade is tirade. The greatest story ever told has become the greatest story never told, or as another colleague puts it, "the greatest story half told." It's time again to tell the whole Jesus story and sing our song again: "This Is

Our Story, This Is Our Song." Maybe it's even time for a whole new missional order in the Wesleyan Way.

He who sings frightens away his ills.
—*Miguel de Cervantes*

But this means Jesus must become the *cantus firmus*, the enduring melody of our lives. When I first began posting on Facebook, I thought I'd have a little fun. So I posted this question: "It's been said that Methodists cry, 'Fire! Fire!' I wonder what other denominations cry?"

The postings on my Wall came fast and furious:

Baptists cry, "Water! Water!"
Episcopalians cry, "Ice! Ice!"
Presbyterians cry, "Order! Order!"
Quakers keep silence.
Lutherans cry, "Beer! Beer!"
Orthodox cry all those things but in threes.
Nazarenes cry, "Potluck! Potluck!"
Fundamentalists cry, "Heresy! Heresy!"
Pentecostals just cry!
UCCers cry, "Quit your crying. . . . God is still speaking."
Post-postmoderns cry, "Why is everybody crying?"
Unitarians cry, "Whatever! Whatever!"
Catholics cry, "Bingo! Bingo!"

The exercise came to an abrupt end when one of my friends posted this: "I wonder who's crying, 'Jesus, Jesus!'" It has become fashionable to refashion Methodism into more-relevant garb. I really don't care whether this book chimes with postmodern tastes or not. People of the Wesleyan tribe, or in Wesley's preferred and deliberate phrasing, "people called Methodists,"[13] it's time to show some originality. In its truest sense, "originality" means a return to origins or a rediscovery of one's roots, not merely to reproduce the current original, which is self-extinction, but to recapitulate the original in the current context, a fresh choreography for daily life of an old dance.

How difficult, though it seems so easy, is it to contemplate a noble disposition, a fine picture, simply in and for itself; to watch the music for the music's sake; to admire the actor in the actor; to take pleasure in a building for its own peculiar harmony and durability.
—Johann Wolfgang von Goethe[14]

Originality that rings true is a palimpsest of past and present. It includes the greatest living and dead singers and choreographers in the circle, enriching the quality of our dance. Kenneth Clark answered the question "What Makes a Masterpiece?" in this way: "a power of recreating traditional forms so that they become expressive of the artist's own epoch, and yet keep a relationship with the past."[15] One of the greatest thinkers about creativity of the twentieth century, Arthur Koestler, testified to his own maturity of thinking about the nature of originality and innovation:

Since my schooldays I have not ceased to marvel each year at the fool I had been the year before. Each year brought its own revelation and each time I could only think with shame and rage of the opinions I had held and vented before the last initiation. This is still true today, but in a modified form. I am still unable to understand how I was able to bear last year's state of profound ignorance, but lately the new revelations instead of shattering and destroying all that went before, seem to combine into a pattern sufficiently elastic to absorb the new material and yet with a certain consistency in its basic features.[16]

When end and beginning meet, either nothing has happened or everything is happening. True originality is a refocusing of the religious imagination, not on the new, but on the old.

Our original song is not a song of "Here I am" but a song of "There's the *I AM*" as we point to Jesus. Methodism is a masterpiece because it seeks not to create its own song or go its own way, but to rediscover the Master Creator's song and sing it with new instrumentation in a new sacred landscape.

Folksinger Pete Seeger distilled all of the world's knowledge into a single word: *maybe*. Under stress, doubt, uncertainty, and "maybeness," people revert to type, to sop, to the familiar. It is hard to innovate in a spirit of maybe-ness and fear. Fear is contagious. Fear is paralyzing. Fear is a self-fulfilling prophecy: "Truly the thing that I fear comes upon me, and what I dread befalls me."[17]

Why are you afraid? Have you still no faith?
—Jesus[18]

The opposite of a spirit of fear is a spirit of Christ. The spirit of Christ has the power to resurrect, renew, jump-start, jolt. Martin Luther is famous for many statements, but one of his best known is this one: "The Holy Spirit is no skeptic." He went on to say in words that Wesley echoed, "It is not doubts or mere opinions that he has written on our hearts, but assertions more sure and certain than life itself."[19] The mark of the work of the Spirit is not speculation but full assurance. The Holy Spirit brings us truth, not speculation; theology, not moralisms; a bold spirit rather than a hesitant or hit-the-sack spirit. If you're not coping with impossibles, you're not living by faith, for faith traffics in the impossible, not the possible. Faith is able to leap chasms that reason cannot fathom.

In this book, we will sound the negative only in the context of how we can still sing the Lord's song in a land of dissonant, dissenting voices. Where the Western world puts all of its eggs into a "maybe" basket of knowledge, God distills all the world's truth into a single person, One Word made flesh that translates as a different single word: *yes*. Jesus is "God's 'Yes!'" Or as Paul assured the church at Corinth: "Our message to you is not 'Yes' and 'No.' For the Son of God, Jesus Christ, . . . was not 'Yes' and 'No,' but in him it has always been 'Yes.'"[20]

Like Robin Williams in *Dead Poets Society*, in the scene where he has the students tear textbooks and stand on top of desks and speak at the top of their lungs, in this book I'm back to my "shouting Methodist" roots and yelling as loud as I can: "Wake up, church! Do it again, Lord!" In our current competing tides of globalization and tribalization, when a retribalized neo-Calvinism is ascendant, replacing "maybe" with a condemnatory TULIP fundamentalism, perhaps it is time to resurrect a neo-Wesleyan identity and to challenge the prevailing "maybe Methodism," the "one-calorie Methodism" or "diet Methodism" that characterizes so much of our tribe today.

I am not afraid that the people called Methodists should ever cease to exist either in Europe or America. But I am afraid lest they should only exist as a dead sect, having the form of religion without the power. And this undoubtedly will be the case unless they hold fast both the doctrine, spirit, and discipline with which they first set out.
—John Wesley[21]

CHAPTER ONE

THE SONG
OF WATER

*"Lift Up Your Voice
with Strength":
Holiness and Practice*

> *Our life contains a thousand springs,*
> *And dies if one be gone.*
> *Strange! that a harp of thousand strings*
> *Should keep in tune so long.*
> —Isaac Watts, *Hymns* (1707)[1]

Bell, Book, and Candle once symbolized exclusion from church. What symbolizes incorporation into it? Table and Font. For Methodists, the sacraments are not magic but mercies of re-membering and membership.

Water is a cleansing ritual, making baptism a sacramental as well as a covenantal ritual for the tribe of Methodists. To be administered by "washing, dipping, or sprinkling," as John Wesley put it himself, "by baptism, we enter into covenant with God, that everlasting covenant . . . [and] are admitted into the church, and consequently made members of Christ, . . . made children of God. . . . By water, then, as a mean, the water of baptism, we are regenerated or born again."[2] No wonder water is a favorite symbol in Wesley hymns.

But water has another meaning for Methodism. Early Methodist preachers followed the water flow, through mountains and across chasms, because that's where the settlements were. Today, we are still following the water flow, this time across oceans and over continents. Four percent of the world's Christians live in the United States, 96 percent do not. You can't know Christianity by the 4 percent. The same is true of Methodism. There are many more non-English-speaking, non-American Methodist churches throughout the world than exist in the United States. The fastest-growing and largest Methodist churches are non-Western and non-English-speaking.

Everything in the water moves by sound and communicates in sound. What brought masses to the Methodist waters was that they heard the reverberation of Christ's voice and the origins of covenantal identity echoing through the waves of aurality. Methodists were a people of sound mind.

We now know what David the psalmist knew first: the healing powers of sound. We now know what David didn't know: that music can change the cellular environment of a body. For good reason Stalin banned the saxophone in the Soviet Union in 1949, fearing jazz music's subversive spirit of free expression and liberation.[3]

The first time I read D. H. Lawrence's reminiscences about the power of the songs he learned in church and Sunday school when he was a boy, I knew what he was talking about (even though it was a Congregationalist chapel and not a Methodist church). In what has been called one of his "most original essays," Lawrence testified to how these old hymns "live and glisten in the depths of [our adult] consciousness in undimmed wonder, because they have not been subjected to any criticism or analysis."[4] Lawrence testifies not only to the shaping power of these songs of our childhood, but to the way in which faith is made real in the imagination, long before any of it has been fully explained or illuminated: "The Lake of Galilee! I don't want to know where it is. I never want to go to Palestine. Galilee is one of those lovely glamorous worlds, not places, that exists in the golden haze of a child's half-formed imagination. And in my man's imagination it is just the same. It has been left untouched."[5]

I was born and bathed in the waters of Methodism. *Wesleyan* is something I was, not something I belonged to. I entered the faith by the ear-gate. The ears, not the eyes, were the gateways to my soul.[6] My pedigree is about as Methodist as you can get.

I'm a PK. But the preacher in our household was my mother, an Appalachian revivalist named Mabel Velma Boggs, who was ordained in the Pilgrim Holiness Church (I call this tribe the Marine Corps of Methodism). She attended "God's Bible School" in Cincinnati for one year, the same school that educated William Seymour for one year before he went west to start the Azusa Street Revival decades earlier. She left the humbly named school when her favorite professor switched institutions to teach at Allentown Bible College (ABC) in Allentown, Pennsylvania. She graduated from ABC a few years later, and began revival preaching and church planting in the upper regions of the South where "catchers" meant something more than baseball. We buried my preacher-mom at the Wesleyan church in Covington, Virginia, which she had helped plant. She was its first pastor.

While preaching at a revival in Newport News, Virginia, my "single-forever," mid-thirties mother met my Yankee father. At one service, this Army–Air Force sergeant from the foothills of the Adirondack Mountains found his heart "strangely warmed"—but by the preacher as much as the preaching. The shy, quiet Leonard Lucius Sweet, also in his mid-thirties, was assigned to radar operation and stationed at Newport News after the Second World War.

*Mortals join the mighty chorus
Which the morning stars began.*
—Henry van Dyke's *"Joyful, Joyful" (1907),
set to Ludwig van Beethoven's
"Ode to Joy" melody,
from his Ninth Symphony*[7]

On the Sweet side, I come from a different holiness wing of Wesleyanism. My grandfather Ira Sweet was so committed to the Gloversville (New York) Free Methodist Church that, in lean years, he would personally visit prominent businessmen in town to get donations of coal to heat the church. He was a glove cutter by day. But after long twelve- to sixteen-hour days at Fosdick Gloves, he was a lay theologian by night. His library of texts on Wesley, holiness theology, and apocalyptic literature was the envy of many preachers. When he completed reading each book, he entered the date with some notations of what he had learned and jotted down pages of where he wanted to go back. I have some of his library, and many books have two or three dates and notations. I also have the small chair—hard and unupholstered to keep him reading for as long as possible—on which he sat while reading into the wee hours of the morning. As he read, Grandfather Sweet was known for humming hymns and rocking his right ankle forward and backward on the lowest rung of the wooden chair, keeping in beat with the music until he wore down the wood with his shoe to a level so paper-thin, it's a wonder it never broke.

My maternal ancestry is mainstream Methodist, with a decidedly southern Appalachian flavor. My West Virginia grandfather, George Lemuel Boggs, was a sawyer, as were four of his brothers, all of whom were Methodist. I still remember an old ditty my grandfather Boggs would sing as he cut down trees or built birdhouses. I memorized it as a kid because Granddad's nose was always running, and it became a game for my brothers and me to see how far into the song he'd get before that little drop that formed on the tip of his nose would drip down onto what he was sawing and hammering:

> A Methodist, a Methodist will I be
> A Methodist will I die.
> I've been baptized in the Methodist way
> And I'll live on the Methodist side.[8]

What "genius" of Methodism inspired this kind of love and loyalty in earlier days? What did it mean to be baptized in "the Methodist way" and to live on "the Methodist side"? Most important but most easy to miss, why was he *singing* his pledge of allegiance to Methodism? I don't ever remember him reciting it as part of some litany, or recounting it as some mission statement he had learned in vacation Bible school or Sunday school. He whistled and hummed it.

Perhaps my favorite book on the history of Methodism is David Hempton's brilliant and beautifully written *Methodism*. What most readers and reviewers have missed from Hempton's masterful collection, however, is that unlike every other historian, Hempton acknowledges in a long paragraph buried in chapter 3 the acoustical architecture and atmosphere of Methodism. Although a paragraph is not enough, Hempton recognizes that Methodism was largely an oral movement, and he builds on the work of Leigh Eric Schmidt to contend that it is hard for historians whose instruments are primarily written to grasp the oral character of the movement. Our acoustical antennae "are simply not adjusted to hearing the religious sounds of the past the way they were heard at the time."[9] Hempton also might have mentioned that the soundscape of the past was very different from the soundscapes of the twenty-first century—filled as they are now with ringtones and playlists and squeaking traffic. In fact, it was not very long ago that village life was governed by a soundscape largely regulated by religion: the pealing of church bells primarily; although street preachers, organ-grinders, and sidewalk vendors added their hellos and halloos.

Critics of Wesley used the phrase "nonsense and noise" to decry the enthusiasm and emotion associated with Methodists. We should have listened to these cries more carefully in assessing Methodism's success in "making Christianity a mass enterprise."[10] By "rejecting the standard reformed sermon as a read discourse with a stiff theological spine," Nathan Hatch argues, "Methodists crafted sermons that were audience-centered, vernacular, and extemporaneous."[11] One can only wonder if this fundamental reality is something seminary faculties missed in the evolution of Methodist preaching in the twentieth century, as they returned it to a respectable literary discourse rather than an oral experience. John Wesley knew how to strum an audience like an instrument. His sermons communicated at an emotional level beyond words. Get the music right, and you capture the crowd. When the crowd, musician, and music become one, you have a revival.

The secret that unlocks the power of Methodism is its "noise," or what I call its sound theology.

Sound is the primary way of experiencing the divine, and Methodism makes no sense without that word *experience*. Methodism was built on sound, and Methodists created a soundscape for experiencing the Christian life that has not been equaled, much less excelled.

Nothing is without sound.
—Apostle Paul[12]

The legacy of that soundscape is still with us whenever we sing a Wesleyan hymn. Just as Frank Sinatra was known simply as "The Voice," John Wesley was "The Voice" of the Wesleyan movement. But no one today remembers a John Wesley sermon. What we all do remember, however, are Charles Wesley's hymns. We remember musical melodies more than we do prose passages. The human brain is wired for sound.

For his entire life, John kept moving and supporting the movement on horseback. After Charles married, unlike John, he settled down. But Charles, whom some call "the first Methodist," kept moving and supporting the movement in his own way. Charles wrote an astonishing number of hymns (6,500–9,000), equal to the astonishing number of horseback miles his brother racked up (250,000), or the even more astonishing number of sermons John delivered (40,000).

The Wesleys first discovered the power of congregational hymn singing while on a voyage with twenty-six German Moravians to Georgia in 1735. It wasn't the storm that shook Wesley's heart and turned it inside out. Granted, the storm was scary enough. It split the windjammer's mainsail and broke the mast in two. Passengers were running hither and yon, scrambling for cover—except for the Moravians.

They calmly kept on singing. The stronger the winds howled, the louder they sang; and the louder they sang, the stronger their faith. What so moved Wesley was not the fierceness of the storm, but the singing in the storm. Not the song in the storm, but their singing in the storm is what drew him to a deeper faith. Later, at a Moravian meetinghouse in London, he would give himself fully to Jesus.

The immediate result was John Wesley's publication in 1737 of his *Collection of Psalms and Hymns*, the first hymnal printed in America and the first significant Wesley publication. Between 1738 and 1785, the Wesleys published sixty-four separate collections of hymns, wherein John's chief role was translating songs from German and selecting, editing, and publishing his brother's hymns.

The Wesleys' commitment to hymns was an acknowledgment of the endurance and strength of God's healing song within the turbulence and uncertainties of life. For both John and Charles, that link between faith and life found its roots in a Christ identity that harkened back to the creation itself and found expression in a holistic view of humanness. Good music was good medicine.

John Wesley began his pioneering book of health remedies, *Primitive Physick* (1747), with a testimony to how God initially created us to be in harmony with our Creator and creation: "So that well might the morning stars sing together, and all the sons of God shout for joy."[13] In Wesley's holistic approach to health, which issued in one of the most popular volumes published in England during the eighteenth century, "salvation" and "health" were identical.[14] The Fall broke that harmony of body, spirit, and soul, in which "all nature sings, and round me rings, the music of the spheres."[15] The rift between Creator and creation led to all kinds of sadness and illness and wickedness that were the result of inharmonious relationships. The song of the body is restored when "chords that were broken will vibrate once more," in the words of Fanny Crosby.[16]

Harry Mark Petrakis (b. 1923) is a Greek American novelist who has written twenty-three novels. One of them, *A Dream of Kings*, was made into a major motion picture starring Anthony Quinn (1969). In the story, a Greek immigrant named Leonidas Matsoukas lives in Chicago with his wife and three kids and mother-in-law. His son Stavros, whom he loves fiercely, is very sick and hangs on to life by a thread. The doctors tell the family that all the tests reveal Stavros has only months to live. But the father never gives up. He is convinced that if he could only take his son back to his native land and expose him to the Mediterranean sun, he would be healed. One April morning, he speaks to his sleeping, frail son: "The [Chicago] sun has risen but you cannot see or feel it. . . . It is pale and without strength and beneath it even the weeds wither and die. But soon now, my beloved, we will leave this place of dark and rot, soon you will feel the sun of the old country, the sun of Hellas."[17]

He closes his eyes and whispers, "You have never seen a sun like that. . . . It warms the flesh, toughens the heart, purifies the blood in its fire. It will make you well, will burn away your weakness with its flame, will heal you with its grace."[18]

This is how the Hebrew prophet Malachi put it about the Messiah: "But for you who revere my name the sun of righteousness shall rise, with healing in its wings."[19] Or how it is expressed in the Wesley hymn based on that text, the greatest hymn of the Incarnation ever written, appropriately coming with a platinum pedigree (lyrics by Charles Wesley [1734], arrangement by George Whitefield [1753], tune by Felix Mendelssohn [1840]): "Hail the heaven-born Prince of Peace! / Hail the Sun of Righteousness! / Light and life to all he brings, / risen with healing in his wings."[20]

Down in the human heart, crushed by the tempter,
Feelings lie buried that grace can restore;
Touched by a loving heart, wakened by kindness,
Chords that were broken will vibrate once more.
—*Fanny Crosby*[21]

Wherever there are Methodists, there is music. Methodism left an acoustic imprint on Christianity that was largely shaped by Charles, who called his hymns "a body of experimental and practical divinity."[22] But others like Isaac Watts (1674–1748), whom John Wesley deemed a genius, deeply influenced Methodism's sound theology—although Isaac Watts maintained that Charles Wesley's "Wrestling Jacob" was worth all of his own 750 hymns.[23] John Wesley's role in hymnody through the songs he selected for his various hymnbooks cannot be minimized.

For Charles Wesley, the two most important languages of humanity, theology and music, were one and the same. In other words, his very theological method was an aesthetics of sound,[24] and his music was the essence of the movement, a feature of Methodism that continued into the nineteenth century with the Wesleyan hymn writer Fanny Crosby (1820–1915) and her eight thousand hymns. The Methodist movement was the product of sound architecture.

Since the data we receive from our ears are so much more precise than that from our eyes, and the capacity for transcendence is located in our sense of hearing, you can even make a case for Charles Wesley being the more systematic and sophisticated theologian of the two brothers. Augustine noted in a commentary on the Bible that words tend toward the quality of music, which does not find its being in time and does not have any particular geographical location. Composer Felix Mendelssohn went further. He insisted that "a piece of music that I love expresses thoughts to me that are not too imprecise to be framed in words, but too precise. So I find that attempts to express such thoughts in words may have some points to them but they are also unsatisfying."[25]

What the Wesley brothers had discovered, even though they did not have a nonbiblical language for it, was that at the deepest level, you and I are spirit.[26] The word becomes flesh, or in more contemporary language, spirit matters. Matter is energy; form is relationship; structure is rhythm.

Sound creates structure, not the other way around.

Music, especially sacred music, has a powerful efficacy to soften the heart into tenderness, to harmonize the affections, and to give the mind a relish for objects of a superior character.
—Jonathan Edwards[27]

Methodism's songs of a "thousand tongues" lift the veil of the future described in the book of Revelation, where "the voice of a great multitude, like the sound of many waters"[28] praise God for eternity:

O for a thousand tongues to sing
my great Redeemer's praise,
the glories of my God and King,
the triumphs of his grace!

Jesus! the name that charms our fears,
that bids our sorrows cease;
'tis music in the sinner's ears,
'tis life, and health, and peace.[29]

The whole of Methodism is there in those two stanzas written almost three hundred years ago. The "method" of "Methodism" was music, not mechanics or organization or books of discipline.

When Wesley and some of his followers first arrived at a village or town, their "method" of evangelism was to hit the streets singing Methodist songs until people gathered, and then Wesley would preach. This was the "method" of Methodism. John Wesley would walk the streets of a small English town singing hymns with an entourage of twenty to thirty of his Methodists. They would march to the commons in the center of town, where Wesley would preach a relatively short sermon on living each day as if it were your last *and* first. He would then give an invitation, but the invitation was not to accept Christ (this was pre-evangelism) but the desire to "fear God and flee the wrath to come." Then Wesley's entourage would circulate among those responding to the invitation, signing them up on the spot for a class meeting that afternoon, where the real work of evangelism would take place. The vast majority of people who became followers of Jesus Christ in Wesley "revivals" were converted one-on-one in class meetings.[30]

A translation is no translation unless it will give you the music
of a poem along with the words of it.
—*Irish playwright J. M. Synge (1871–1909)*[31]

Methodism featured an aural aesthetics of the sublime that not only was accessible to the common people but also was powerful enough to bring down the walls of despotism and prejudice. For Methodism, soulfulness is soundfulness. In fact, one of Wesley's favorite descriptions of his congregations was "a listening multitude."[32] Anglicans carry theology in their liturgy. Methodists carry theology in their hymns.[33] For Methodism, creeds are best sung as celebrations of faith, not tests of truth or pledges of allegiance to orthodoxy.

The *Book of Discipline* was another form of Wesley's "Directions for Singing." It was a manual for how souls were to be listened to and sounded forth into existence. Not every bud becomes a flower. But every time a bud bursts and a flower is born, a sound is made. So every time a soul is born, a crying is made amid surrounding smiles.

Methodism taught its members to hear the voice of God amid the white noise. Where some heard only deafening thunder and lightning, Methodists heard the voice of an angel.[34] Where some talked of "bad luck" or "good fortune," Methodists traced divine providence. Methodism cascaded hymnbooks and song leaders like other traditions generated creeds and liturgists. Most prominent preachers had their name associated with some hymn, hymnbook, or musician. In 1829, Methodist itinerant Orange Scott, later founder of the Wesleyan Methodists, published a controversial "Camp Meeting Hymn Book" that excluded a lot of "favorites" because he deemed them "destitute, either of good sense, good poetry, or sound divinity."[35]

This is my Father's world,
And to my listening ears
all nature sings, and round me rings
the music of the spheres. . . .

This is my Father's world,
the birds their carols raise,
the morning light, the lily white,
declare their maker's praise.

This is my Father's world:
he shines in all that's fair;
in the rustling grass I hear him pass;
he speaks to me everywhere.
—Maltbie D. Babcock (1901)[36]

In the last sentence of his magical paragraph, Professor Hempton puts it like this: "The Methodist message was inexorably bound up with the medium of oral culture. Itinerants preached, exhorters exhorted, class members confessed, hymns were sung, prayers were spoken, testimonies were delivered, and revival meetings throbbed with exclamatory noise."[37] He forgot to mention the "praise meetings" Methodists called "shouts."

THIS IS OUR STORY, THIS IS OUR SONG

In fact, in the early days of Methodism in America, the name most often used to describe the movement was not "Methodists" but "shouting Methodists." Methodists embraced this name as a badge of distinction: "I do believe, without a doubt / The Christian has a right to shout" was one early Methodist mantra.[38] In Stith Mead's Methodist songbook of 1807, *Hymns and Spiritual Songs*, there is the famous "Shouting Methodist" song that was placed in the cornerstone of Foundry Methodist Church in Washington, D.C. But at the time it was simply titled "The Methodist," and it went like this:

> The World, the Devil, and Tom Paine
> Have try'd their force, but all in vain.
> They can't prevail, the reason is,
> The Lord defends the Methodist.
>
> They pray, they sing, they preach the best,
> And do the Devil most molest.
> If Satan had his vicious way,
> He'd kill and damn them all today.

13

They are despised by Satan's train,
Because they shout and preach so plain.
I'm bound to march in endless bliss,
And die a shouting Methodist.[39]

An alternate second stanza won out for obvious reasons, although the last syllable of "Methodist" was twisted so it could rhyme with "increase":

They pray the most, they preach the best
They labor most for endless rest
I hope my Lord will them increase
And fill the world with Methodist.[40]

The term *shouting Methodist* symbolized the rich aural culture of Methodism. Sermons were interactive, participatory experiences filled with sonic explosions from the congregation in the vernacular of the common people: "Praise the Lord," "Hallelujah," "Amen," and "Glory!" Alexander Campbell reported with amazement how Methodism's "periodical *Amens* dispossess demons—storm heaven—shut the gates of hell—and drive Satan from the camp."[41] No service would have been counted worship without singing and shouting, laughing and crying, extemporaneous praying and exhorting, clapping and stomping, which sometimes turned to dancing. If dance is a way of organizing space and time, usually in relationship to music, then Methodists were dance masters, even though they frowned on dancing outside of worship. A day I don't dance, or shout, is a day I don't live.

I think everyone should sing all the time. If the good Lord gave you a beautiful singing voice, it's a fine way to say "thank you." If he never did, it's a good way to get even.
—*Cowboy singer/songwriter Van Holyoak*[42]

In the same songbook of 1807, a convert to Methodism gives his initial impression:

> The Methodists were preaching like thunder all about.
> At length I went amongst them, to hear them groan and shout.
> I thought they were distracted, such fools I'd never seen.
> They'd stamp and clap and tremble, and wail and cry and scream.[43]

By mid-century, Methodists were a tamer lot. There is an old Presbyterian proverb: "A Methodist is a Baptist who has been taught to read." The Methodist proverb in rejoinder went like this: "A Presbyterian is someone who finds Methodism a bit too racy." We've lost that raciness, along with the rest of mainstream-gone-lamestream Protestantism. All too often, the old-time religion has become "sometime religion" rather than "lifetime religion."

But in the mid-nineteenth century, Methodists were still known for the "noise" of their shouting assemblies. Methodists were famous for the thunder and lightning of their praying (the thunder rolled as the congregation prayed together but individually out loud; the lightning struck when the preacher pierced the din of the people's supplications with new intercessions and directions for prayer). But Methodists were most famous for dying as they "shouted to glory." The Methodist songbook *The Hesperian Harp* (1848) presents a "dialogue song" between a "Methodist" and a "Formalist," in which the "Formalist" gives this passionate picture of a Methodist:

Methodist
> Good morning, brother Pilgrim! What, trav'ling to Zion?
> What doubts and what dangers have you met to-day?
> Have you gain'd a blessing, then pray without ceasing,
> Press forward, my brother and make no delay;
> Is your heart now glowing, your comforts now flowing,
> And have you an evidence now bright and clear?
> Have you a desire that burns like a fire,
> And longs for the hour when Christ shall appear?

15

Formalist

> I came out this morning, and now I'm returning,
> Perhaps little better than when I first came,
> Such groaning and shouting, it sets me to doubting,
> I fear such religion is only a dream.
> The preachers were stamping, the people were jumping,
> And screaming so loud that I nothing could hear,
> Either praying or preaching—such horrible shrieking!
> I was truly offended at all that was there.

Methodist

> Perhaps, my dear brother, while they prayed together
> You sat and considered, but prayed not at all:
> Would you find a blessing, then pray without ceasing,
> Obey the advice that was given by Paul.
> For if you should reason at any such season,
> No wonder if Satan should tell in your ear,
> That preachers and people are only a rabble,
> And this is no place for reflection and prayer.

Formalist

> No place for reflection—I'm filled with distraction,
> I wonder that people could bear for to stay,
> The men they were bawling, the women were squalling,
> I know not for my part how any could pray.
> Such horrid confusion—if this be religion
> I'm sure that it's something that never was seen,
> For the sacred pages that speak of all ages,
> Do nowhere declare that such ever has been.

Methodist

> Don't be so soon shaken—if I'm not mistaken
> Such things were perform'd by believers of old;
> When the ark was coming, King David came running,
> And dancing before it, in Scripture we're told.
> When the Jewish nation had laid the foundation,
> To rebuild the temple at Ezra's command,
> Some wept and some praised, such noise there was raised,
> 'Twas heard afar off and perhaps through the land.
> And as for the preacher, Ezekiel the teacher,
> God taught him to stamp and to smite with the hand,
> To show the transgressions of that wicked nation
> To bid them repent and obey the command.

For Scripture collation in this dispensation,
The blessed Redeemer has handed it out—
"If these cease from praising" we hear him there saying,
"The stones to reprove them would quickly cry out."

Formalist

Then Scripture's contrasted, for Paul has protested
That order should reign in the house of the Lord—
Amid such a clatter who knows what's the matter?
Or who can attend unto what is declared?
To see them behaving like drunkards, all raving,
And lying and rolling prostrate on the ground,
I really felt awful, and sometimes felt fearful
That I'd be the next that would come tumbling down.

Methodist

You say you felt awful—you ought to be careful
Lest you grieve the Spirit, and so he depart,
By your own confession you've felt some impression,
The sweet melting showers have soften'd your heart.
You fear persecution, and that's a delusion
Brought in by the devil to stop up your way.
Be careful, my brother, for blest are no other
Than persons that "are not offended in Me."
As Peter was preaching, and bold in his teaching,
The plan of salvation in Jesus' name,
The Spirit descended and some were offended,
And said of these men, "They're filled with new wine."
I never yet doubted that some of them shouted,
While others lay prostrate, by power struck down;
Some weeping, some praising, while others were saying:
"They're drunkards or fools, or in falsehood abound."
As time is now flying and moments are dying,
We're call'd to improve them, and quickly prepare
For that awful hour when Jesus, in power
And glory is coming—'tis now drawing near.
Methinks there'll be shouting, and I'm not a-doubting,
But crying and screaming for mercy in vain;
Therefore, my dear brother, let us pray together,
That your precious soul may be fill'd with the flame.

Formalist

I own prayers now needful, I really feel awful

That I've grieved the Spirit in time that is past;
But I'll look to my Savior, and hope to find favor,
The storms of temptation will not always last.
I'll strive for the blessing, and pray without ceasing,
His mercy is sure unto all that believe.
My heart is now glowing! I feel his love flowing!
Peace, pardon, and comfort I now do receive![44]

The "Formalist" did come tumbling down. His heart was "glowing," Christ's love was "flowing," and "peace, pardon, and comfort" he found.[45]

Sing lustily and with a good courage. Beware of singing as if you were half dead, or half asleep; but lift up your voice with strength. . . . Do not bawl, so as to be heard above or distinct from the rest of the congregation, that you may not destroy the harmony; but strive to unite your voices together.
—John Wesley, "Directions for Singing" (1761)[46]

Of course, the "noise" was "nonsense" only to those who prejudged the sound, to those who looked without listening to class meetings, love feasts, testimony times, camp meetings, revival services, and the abundance of diverse sounds in which these Methodists surrounded themselves. The real genius of Methodism was in how it transformed noise into music, and trained its members to hear the music in the harshest places and most tragic circumstances. Methodism re-pivoted Western spirituality in a more Eastern direction by emphasizing sacred sound as much as sacred time, sacred space, and sacred image. More than any other Christian movement, Methodists were the embodiment of *fides et auditu*. It was Methodist "faith [that] comes by hearing, and hearing by the word."[47] Cut a Methodist, and they bleed musical notes.

The Wesleys were not the first to grasp the sonic realm of spirituality. There is the chanting of the Hebrews, the Gregorian chants of the

Roman church, the "Jesus Prayer" chants of the Eastern Orthodox church. But only Methodism was built from the sound up. Only in Methodism was faith less a "vision" thing than a "vibration" thing. Methodists were masters where others were misers of sound and syllable. The Wesleyan movement bathed its members in vibrations of the holy, and offered a song for every struggle of life, a sound track for every heartache of human existence.

What is the sound of a Methodist heart breaking? It's a song that goes like this:

> Jesus, lover of my soul, / let me to thy bosom fly, / while the nearer waters roll, / while the tempest still is high. / Hide me, O my Savior, hide, / till the storm of life is past; / safe into the haven guide; / O receive my soul at last.[48]

The human panorama of generosity and greed, complicity and loss, success and failure, life and death were covered in song, thereby putting music into the health regimen of every human being.

What won the hearts of the people was not Wesley's expository notes or doctrinal treatises or dynamic preaching. Rather, Methodism provided a new, sacred soundscape and metaphorical universe for the living out of daily life in a new social landscape. Methodists were people who sang their lives.

There is a well-known collection of prayers from the Western Isles of Scotland called the *Carmina Gadelica*, Latin for "The Songs of the Gaels." Translated from Gaelic into English, these are songs and incantations that people would be singing as they performed their daily routines. Here is the blessing while churning the butter:

> Thou Who put beam in moon and sun,
> Thou Who put food in ear and herd,
> Thou Who put fish in stream and sea,
> Send the butter up betimes.[49]

Methodists may not have had songs for the churning of the butter. But they had songs for almost everything else, including a child cutting his teeth. And it was this soundscape that encased daily spiritual equipment for living that captured Anglo-American cultures, making the nineteenth century in American history become known as "The Methodist Age" and capturing popular culture like no other tribe has done before or since.[50] You might even say that nineteenth-century Methodism was the closest the United States ever came to having a state church.

John and Charles Wesley rediscovered the musical language of Pentecost where sound becomes sight, the invisible becomes visible, vibration becomes vision. Only after the sound of "a rushing mighty wind" filled the room did the "tongues, as of fire" become visible."[51] Like any language, especially the English language, depending on where you live and where you're from, Methodism had a different accent, used different words, phrases, and punctuation. Methodism could even sound different.[52] But it was always the same method that produced the same song of a thousand tongues.

METHOD-ISM AND MUSIC

There is an old film about the laws of sound that shows a handful of iron filings placed on a thin sheet of metal. A musical tone was played near the sheet. Suddenly the filings arranged themselves in the form of a snowflake. Sound became sight, as vibrations took physical shape. Another tone was sounded, and the filings changed their formation— this time into a star.

Every note sounded created its own physical form. The invisible became visible.

Angels are intermediaries between heaven and earth, between the invisible and the visible. Sound is an angelic force in life because sound moves things from the invisible to the visible, from the physical to the spiritual, from spirit into matter.[53] And if spirit can become matter through sound, then matter can become spirit again through song.

An idea can transform the world
and rewrite all the rules
—Dominic "Dom" Cobb ("The Extractor") in Inception[54]

The gospel is an idea that can transform the world and rewrite the rules. Music is a medium that can transpose the gospel into a powerful and beautiful message. But great music requires great preparation. Music is a combination drill and gift, mechanics and emotion, movement and stasis, sound and silence.

Music and method always go together. Music is the art of method, not free-form lawlessness or freedom from constraints. Methodism was method music for the masses. The Methodist Song involved a practiced method of musical theology that was accessible to all. It provided a path and power for releasing the music within each of us. Just as musical method and theory features disciplines of scales, fingering, exercises, keys, rhythm, fluency, dynamics, articulation, and transposition, the Methodist method of theology through song featured disciplines of originality, play, pitch, silence, and breathing. For Methodists, there is a progression in difficulty and stages of development, for which John Wesley believed God raised up "the people called Methodist" in the first place—a sanctification process in holiness that was accomplished through "practice."[55]

The acoustic scale of Methodism featured five tracks that tick into one valence. Put into nonmusical, more organic language, Methodism involved an ecology of methods that collectively formed a unified ecosystem of "practice-makes-perfect" discipleship. There might be disagreement over the constituent features of that ecosystem, but there was no disagreement over the need to put the discipline in discipleship.

1. DISCIPLINES OF ORIGINALITY

We are each an original, one-of-a-kind song. Every human being is an original composition by the Master Composer. No song—no matter how successful, powerful, fancy, or famous—is of more value than any other song. Some are of more service than others, to be sure, but none are of more value. All songs are of equal value.

In fact, each one of us is born a child prodigy, an artist. But in the process of "growing up," the prodigy artist vanishes along with the innocence of childhood. That song inside of you wanting to come out becomes lost or stolen or altered. Like the baby swan that yearns to be a duckling, not realizing its own exquisite form, our growth into adulthood can alter our sense of beauty and self-perception and can morph our desire to become a bigger, more mature *me* into the desire to become a bigger, more mature *other.*

My favorite Winnie-the-Pooh great adventure is when Winnie-the-Pooh and Tigger too look all over the Hundred Acre Wood for Winnie's song. Eventually, Winnie realizes where the song is hidden: the song is within Tigger's heart. In his own "Tigger Song," the bouncy, boisterous tiger with the springy tail sings about what is the most wonderful thing about himself: "I'm the only one."

The greatest developmental task of every human being is to discover your original "I'm-the-only-one" song and sing it ravishingly to the glory of God. Discipleship is fundamentally human formation and song discovery. Discipleship is more than following a method. Discipleship is finding the song that God made us to be, as each one of us is a strand of sound that choruses together to sing the Maker's hymn of praise. The greatest joy in life comes from helping people find the notes to their song. Or just listen to their song.

How do you find your song? By listening to the voice within and the way your voice harmonizes with the voices around you. By nudging others to find and sing their song, by strumming others like an instrument, you encourage others to find their song too. This is called evangelism, which is another word for discipleship. Scholar Judith Maizel-Long's study of the Methodist hymnbook chronicles the decrease of evangelism during the twentieth century. Where Wesley's 1780 hymnbook was organized around "evangelism as the organizing principle," by 1904 the rationale of Methodist hymnody was no longer mission but "handbooks for Christian life within the church."[56]

Maybe it's time Methodism too rediscovered its song, and recovered its voice. Culture is song, including a tribal culture, and when a culture like Methodism no long breaks out in song, there is an identity crisis.

Soyez réglé dans votre vie et ordinaire comme un bourgeois,
afin d'être violent et original dans vos œuvres.
Be regulated and ordinary in your life like a bourgeois,
so that you may be violent and original in your life's work.
—*French novelist Gustave Flaubert (1821–80)*[57]

Humans are the only species who pass up being what they are made to be. Why is that? How do we lose our song? Who steals our song?

Our song is stolen from us by jealousy: "My sister sings better than I do. She's got a better voice, and her pitch is near perfect. Why didn't God give me her voice?"

Our song is stolen from us by hoarding the sound for ourselves. "I only sing in the shower where no one can hear me. I don't sing in public and share my music."

Our song is stolen from us by fear—fear of rejection, fear of hitting wrong notes, fear of not measuring up or keeping up. Mountains aren't measured in feet, but in increments of fear. Even when the song has not been muffled, many people's songs have modulated into fugues of fear and despair.

Our song is stolen from us by shame: "Is that the best you can come up with? I've heard that song a thousand times. Your brother can sing better than that."

> Lord, I've been in hell so long,
> Thank you for helping me out,
> You've given me a brand new song;
> You mapped the whole road out.
> —SanDee Whitfield Tillee[58]

You will have, someday, one last day as yourself. If you're a Methodist, you sing your own song on that last day. Yours only, and no one else's. But on that day, you will not only know the words to your song, you will know the experience of your song serving and blending with God's symphony of life.[59]

That was part of the meaning of John Wesley's boast, "Our people die well."[60]

2. DISCIPLINES OF PLAY

You don't work a violin. You play a violin. Play is what makes discipleship an art.

> Everything in the world plays: the blood in the veins of a lover,
> the sun on the water, and the musician on a violin. Everything
> good in life—love, nature, art and domestic puns—is play.
> —Vladimir Nabokov, addressing a Russian
> literary circle (1925)[61]

Everyone who walks through the doors of the church is a person who is learning to "play" his or her life, faith, and love. *Playing* is the right metaphor. You "play" the piano. You "play basketball." The greatest artistry comes not from "work" but from "play."

Play is serious business. But art is conceived out of play faster than work. That's why the highest expressions of beauty and artistry come out of a play paradigm, not a work ethic. "Works of art" are better named "plays of art," since they come not from "work" but from "play."

According to some historians, the "Protestant work ethic" was an invention of the Calvinist doctrine of predestination. See if you can follow this line of reasoning. Calvinists introduced the question of "Am I saved? Am I not saved?" You don't really know fully, and never can fully know. But the fact that you are saved means you live in a godly way. So everybody wants to show that they are saved by living a godly life. The subconscious urge to prove election got Protestants up early to work their buns off for economic acquisition and worldly success.[62]

I never really did understand the logic behind this ideological complicity between Calvinism and capitalism, although I am comforted to know that ideas, even theology, influence economics. It seemed to be that the same logic could produce an ethic of laziness as much as a mulish work ethic.

The lazy ass breaks its back with work.
—German proverb

But the Methodists offered another ethic, based not on the doctrine of predestination, but on the theology of the garden. Wesley would not have called it a "play paradigm," for that word *play* was too associated in the eighteenth-century mind with what today we would call "amusements." And Wesley associated that word with "idleness" and "laziness." That's why when Wesley started the Kingswood School (1748), he outlawed "play time," by which he meant stagnant space in the day to be filled in by playing cards and other forms of spiritually and morally lazy entertainments. Wesley himself was a lover of the arts, especially the musical and dramatic arts. Charles Wesley may have convinced the wife of the proprietor of Covent Gardens to renounce the theater, but "Love Divine, All Loves Excelling" was Charles's appropriation of Henry Purcell's theater music to Christian theology. As one musicologist has written, "The brothers borrowed melodies from folk-tunes, German songs, and popular plays, such as John Gay's *The Beggar's Opera*."[63]

But the greatest artistic achievements in life for Methodism came out of the relational arts. In the Wesleyan tradition, aesthetics is based on the quality of relational connections, not the quality of artistic commodities. For Wesley, missionary activity in the mines and prisons and hovels was sheer artistry, even meditation in motion.

There is something to be said for the notion of work as either punishment or penance. In fact, the work paradigm is what humanity got in the expulsion from the garden. God created us to continue God's creative play in creation, and the work paradigm only entered the picture when humanity rejected God's project for its own. The Italian word *sprezzatura* is untranslatable, but the essence of its meaning is this: if you look like you're "hard at it," you haven't practiced enough.

Man only plays when he is in the fullest sense
of the word a human being, and he is only fully
a human being when he plays.
—German philosopher Friedrich Schiller (1759–1805)

Unlike work, play is done in community and in joy. Wesley called Methodists to a true celebration of life, with anxiety in nothing, thanksgiving in anything, and prayerfulness in everything.[64] Then the peace of God, which passes all understanding, would return us to "the good life" of the garden. "For everything God created is good, and nothing is to be rejected if it is received with thanksgiving."[65] This attitude of trust, gratitude, and prayer issued in a life of rejoicings and risk-takings. There is one thing Jesus never was, and that was boring.[66] To make the divine boring, dull, and lifeless is the ultimate heresy.

Joy is the Christian's inheritance. "'Sour godliness,' so called, is of the devil,"[67] was one of Wesley's signature sayings. Known for his cheerfulness and upbeat spirit, Wesley couldn't stand to be around people whose "mouths" were *not* "filled with laughter, tongues with songs of joy." This does not mean that the life of faith is one unbroken C Major chord of "Happy in Jesus." Jesus was the Lion of the tribe of Judah that roared. But he was also the bleating Lamb that was slain.

> *The early Franciscans, the early Methodists, the early Salvationists—all were exuberantly happy. . . .*
> *So let us meet the world with joy!*
> —W. E. Sangster[68]

To take oneself seriously is to laugh at oneself, not to take oneself solemnly. After all, "our mouths were filled with laughter, our tongues with songs of joy. . . . The LORD has done great things for us, and we are filled with joy."[69] True blasphemy is not to laugh at holy things, but to not laugh at holy things. Laughter is the leading foreshadow of heaven.

If you live with constant criticism, you learn to condemn.
If you live with constant hostility, you learn to fight.

27

> If you live with constant ridicule, you learn to hide.
> If you live with constant shaming, you learn to feel guilty.

But . . .

> If you live with encouragement, you learn to be confident.
> If you live with praise, you learn to be appreciative.
> If you live with tolerance, you learn to be patient.
> If you live with trust, you learn to live by faith.

Methodism is at its best when its humor is at its highest. When a politician asked a retired bishop for some advice, the bishop told the politician to go out into the rain and lift his head heavenward. "It will bring a revelation to you," the bishop promised. The next day the politician reported back: "I followed your advice, Bishop, and no revelation came. Only water pouring down my neck. I felt like a fool." "Well," the bishop said, "isn't that quite a revelation for the first try?" Sometimes the humor takes an ironic twist. The British Methodist preacher William E. Sangster (1900–1960) looked at his congregation one Sunday and said, "Do you realize that there are many who are *not* in church this morning because you *are*?" Every call to worship is a call to celebrate the great joke God played on sin and death by raising Jesus from the dead. If you don't want to join in the praise and gladness celebrating God's love for us, there are other tribes to join. If you'd rather your society be a place of gladiatorial combat rather than glades of gladness, go somewhere else. As John Wesley wrote to Francis Asbury in 1788: "Let the . . . do what they please, but let the Methodists know their calling better."[70]

One of the reasons why Wesley liked Isaac Watts's hymns so much was their drumbeat of joy: "Joy to the world, the Lord is come, . . . And heaven and nature sing" (1719). "Come ye that love the Lord, and let your joys be known; join in a song with sweet accord" (1707).[71] When pressed to define "the character of a Methodist," John Wesley answered, in a 1742 tract of that title, "God is the joy of his heart. . . .

28

He is therefore happy in God, yea, always happy, as having in him 'a well of water springing up into everlasting life,' and 'overflowing his soul with peace and joy.'"[72]

Joy to the earth! The Saviour reigns!
Let men [and women] their songs employ.
While fields and floods, rocks, hills, and plains
Repeat the sounding joy.
—Isaac Watts[73]

If "the joy of the Lord is your strength,"[74] then maybe one reason our tribe is so weak is . . . where's the joy? If there is one thought that drives me to the juniper tree, it is this one: Where's the joy? When did we become such a gloomy group? Wasn't even Jesus criticized for enjoying life a bit too much?

Granted, there doesn't need to be a "ha-ha" before every "aha." But almost. Good humor, humility, and heroic resilience are required to enter truth's temple, not to mention weather the most ordinary life with dignity and compassion. Can any Wesleyan accept what God has in mind for her or him without a sense of humor?

A medieval legend tells of the angel Lucifer, the smartest, shrewdest, most charming of all the angels, who rebelled against the heavenly hosts and found himself banished from home. Setting up a rebel state, Lucifer was convalescing from his fall one day when he was asked about his former life. "I suspect, Lucifer, you suffer from homesickness. What is it you miss most about heaven?"

Lucifer reflected only for a moment. "What I miss most about heaven," he replied, "are the sound of trumpets in the morning."[75] What is missing most in our tribe are those trumpets sounding the joy of Easter in the morning.

The opposite of joy is not sadness, but hardness of heart. In Jesus, a heart of gladness replaces a heart of stone. And that heart of gladness drives us out into the world for unpremeditated participation in the ongoing passion of Christ to turn tombstones into stepping-stones, and millstones into milestones.

Every biography of Wesley attests to Wesley's conviction that when your life is in the mission mode, terms like *work* and *rest* do not apply. *Opus Dei* means "work of God." But for Wesley, something is a "work of God" not only because God does it. An *opus dei* is not a work done by God so much as it is a work done *for* God. God enjoys your being. At the same time, God enjoins your being—for ministry and mission. And nothing is more *opus dei* than another—whether that *opus dei* be washing wounds or washing windows.

Methodists go beyond *opus dei* to *ludens dei*. We less participate in the "work of God" than the "play of God." This is partly what is behind the Wesleyan mantra of "Holiness is happiness." Happiness is not the material consumption of things or the fulfillment of desire. Happiness is pleasing God.

The elderly John Wesley, just a few months shy of his eighty-sixth birthday, asked a crowd of Irish Methodists gathered in Dublin a classic question from an unlikely source: the Westminster Shorter Catechism: "For what end did God create man?"

The Calvinist answer is "to glorify God and enjoy him forever." Wesley insisted that the Methodists' answer was shorter and better and should be "inculcated upon every human creature": You are made to be happy in God.

That's it. Wesley then playfully suggested that every parent should follow in the wake of every child who learns to walk or talk, and whisper in his or her ear, over and over again: "[God] made *you*; and he made you to be happy in him; and nothing else can make you happy."[76]

We were made to experience God's pleasure. Not other people's applause and pleasure, but God's pleasure. To "please God" is to bring pleasure to God. Only in God's presence are found "pleasures forevermore."[77] . . . not in Wall Street or in the American Dream or in Disney world. Only in God's presence.

And what brings God pleasure? The love of God and love of neighbor. Or in Wesley's phrasing, "in two words, gratitude and benevolence; gratitude to our Creator and supreme Benefactor, and benevolence to our fellow creatures."[78] Benefaction issues in beneficence. A grateful heart activates helping hands.

Joy is the serious business of heaven.
—*C. S. Lewis*[79]

---

3. DISCIPLINES OF PITCH

I once heard from Joe Harding the story of the bachelor who loved the color yellow. His apartment was completely furnished in yellow. He had a yellow rug, yellow wallpaper, yellow couch, yellow chairs. His kitchen was completely furnished in yellow. He had a yellow table, yellow refrigerator, yellow stove, yellow dishwasher. His bedroom was all yellow. He had yellow sheets, yellow pillows, yellow bedspread; and he slept in yellow pajamas.

One day he became extremely jaundiced, and he called for a doctor to visit him at home, since he was too sick to go to the office. The apartment manager said, "You will have no problem finding your patient. Just go to the third floor and down the hall to the yellow door."

The doctor was back at the manager's desk in no time. "Were you able to help him?" he asked the physician. "Help him," said the doctor, "I couldn't even find him!"

That's the way the church has become. We have so become "of" the world, and not just "in" it, that we've disappeared against the background of the world. And we wonder that no one can find us? We're invisible. We think, act, live no differently from anyone else in the culture we're in. "*Sieg Heil*" was a mantra and military salute used in greetings and farewells. It literally translates as "Hail Victory." What happens when "*Sieg Heil*" or "Hail Victory" becomes the mantra of an entire culture? What happens when the church's definition of "winning" is no different from the world's? In a culture where if you can't "count" it, it doesn't count, what happens when the world's alphabet of success (the ABCs of Attendance, Buildings, Cash) becomes the church's alphabet?

The world thinks of "winning" as:

> From nobody to UPSTART.
> From upstart to CONTENDER.
> From contender to WINNER.
> From winner to CHAMPION.
> From champion to DYNASTY.[80]

Jesus thinks of "winning" as:

> From nobody to somebody;
> from somebody to everybody;
> from everybody to everything;
> from everything to nothing;
> from nothing to nobody.

May God grant me to become nothing.
—*Simone Weil*[81]

One of my heroes is Buell H. Kazee (1900–1976), a Kentucky Baptist minister and banjo-picker who pastored a church while he composed early country-and-western music; conducted revivals; taught college students; and authored theological books, tracts, and essays. Kazee was so successful at keeping his preaching and revival singing totally separate from his folk artistry that each world didn't know about the other. One scholar of folk music called him "the greatest white male folk singer" of his day.[82] Kazee writes:

> I am coming to the close of my 20th year in the present pastorate. It is not, nor has it ever been, a large pastorate. The church is small and struggling. I have never been recognized as any great personality anywhere. I am just one of the thousands of plodding pastors buried in the small fields of our land, going on in the face of great opposition, both in the church and out, but trying to be faithful where we are called.... [83]
>
> We have a tendency to "glamorize" people who talk as I have written. Those who come to know me will be disappointed in the living example of what I say. Like Elijah, I am a man of like passions such as others, and in my own estimation I am a total failure of what a man of faith should be.[84]

Of course, this is not how the world thinks. But in a world turned upside down by the gospel, "winning" is for losers.

There are some people who never give a single thought to their spiritual lives, much less to "tuning" the instruments that God has implanted within them. These people are "live for the moment," "don't think about tomorrow," "if it feels good, do it" devotees. Those are the ones who cannot even hear the dissonance between "what I want" and doing "the very thing I hate."[85] But none of us can escape from how God made us: musical instruments designed to vibrate according to the resonances of the eternal.

Instruments need tuning. Not so that "we've got to get everyone going in the same direction." That's called a stampede. Rather, we've got to get those "thousand tongues" tuned to the same pitch.

For John Wesley and his descendants, there is one and only one tuning fork to the eternal. That is Jesus the Christ, God's Perfect Pitch. Not too long ago I tweeted this: "Jesus is God's Final Word." Immediately, Jon Kara Shields tweeted back this: "Jesus is God's Final Word . . . reverberating over and over again in an endless overtone at unity with itself." How beautiful is that!

John Wesley preached Christ, prayed Christ, practiced Christ, and praised Christ. Charles Wesley wrote hymns that preached Christ, prayed Christ, practiced Christ, and praised Christ. To be a "real" human being is to be a Jesus-"realized" human being. We are singing the Master Composer's song with Christ through the Spirit, who continues to sing (as a presence) with us in power (Pentecost), enabling us to sing in harmony with others.

How do we ensure that we keep happy in God? How do we practice staying in tune with the voice of the future?

Disciplines of pitch help us to listen more closely to God's voice, to be more aware of God's grace in our lives, to keep our lives in sync with the living Christ. The more we are aware of how our lives resonate with the life of Jesus and God's design for us, the more we can feel "happy in God." John Wesley taught us that to live a sanctified life meant to strive each and every day to live out life in close relationship with the living Lord—to strive to be "perfect" in him. To perfect our lives in Christ means not to fill our lives with a "to-do list" of work projects, but to live out our lives "in tune" with our Creator, to live in the grace and love of Jesus that make us a happy people to sing God's song in the world. Disciplines of pitch allow us especially to perfect that relationship we have with Christ, to come closer and closer to God as we acknowledge Christ's presence in us and seek to live life in harmony with God's dynamic work in the world, work that sounds not like the grinding of wheels but like a bow on a violin—the music of a world created to resonate God.

How can you "practice" your perfect pitch?

a. Turn Open the Spit Valve

When I played the baritone, I had to drain nasty saliva from a "spit valve." We all need a "spit valve" to rid ourselves of the moraines of waste and runoff that come from daily living "in" but not "of" the world's fairground of folly.

The more we play our instrument, the more our sound can get muddled and muted by the plaque of fattening diversions that build up in our souls. We are macerated and emaciated in media. Periodically, we must stop blowing notes and blow out our vessels so that we can channel God's melody without obstruction. When the world becomes overwhelming, and we find it hard to hear our voices, it's time to scour our minds of every uncharity and unclarity. Our instruments need draining through praying, meditating, paying attention, and listening for God's Spirit to play in and through us. Spit valves remove the blockages, the "cheap tunes" that, like persistent earworms, threaten to hold us up and muck up our song.

Whenever life becomes a bit too hard and hurried, and you find it hard to play your song, open the spit valve, drain your instrument, and start again to get a wind of the symphony of the Spirit.

Or if that doesn't work, take a shower bath.

Christ's voice is always echoing.

b. Turn Off Rival Frequencies and Alien Static

Every culture emits background noise that can complement or contradict our inner voice. Sometimes, a certain amount of background noise can be helpful. It can remind us that we live in a world of many voices, that we can sing our best and most beautiful song amid the din of diverse voices.

People suffering from "churchism"[86] especially need background noise. We can suffer from overexposure to the sound of our own voices. We need to get out more, read authors who aren't published by our own publishing houses, and listen to the cultural cacophony. Background noise can break up the tinnitus of the expected and familiar ringing in our ears. When we sing an enriched song amid the clamor of confusion and error, we can turn a few heads, flip a few hearts, quiet a few dissonant sounds, and in general tip people off to the ongoing presence of God in their lives and in the world.

But when crowd noise crescendos so that it drowns out the divine voice, we lose our ability to locate the sounds of our Creator and Redeemer. To be "in but not of" the world requires us not to escape from the sounds of the world but to turn down, turn away, and at times turn off those frequencies that get in the way of our pursuit of perfect pitch. "Do not conform to the pattern of this world."[87]

We who would be a little-j (follower of Jesus) must be nonconformists, voices that pierce through the world's white noise with brilliant and melodic power and block out that which prevents its hearing.

We who would be a little-j (follower of Jesus) must also be masterful listeners, careful to discern God's song in every place and time. Singing the Master Composer's song requires us to listen for other voices singing God's song around us and to harmonize with these songbirds in a chorus of joyful praise.

We who would be a little-j must remember that our culture is not merely a fallen human creation, but a tapestry with God's handprints all over it.

The Holy Spirit gifts each follower with a unique and passionate voice, a sign of Jesus' resurrection identity in the world. To be in tune with the Spirit, we must be in touch with the world, but not in tune with it. We welcome its creative energy that evidences the gifts of the

Holy Spirit while denying its "gifts" of the unholy spirits that interfere with the true music of the spheres. When our "in touch with" the world slides into a wash of "in tune with" the world, we learn ways to say no to love. And we can't hear God saying "I love you."

My grandparents were not hard of hearing so much as they had a hard time hearing each other. My gramma had so many things going on in the background that when my grandad said to her one day, teasingly, "I'm proud of you," she snapped back, "I'm tired of you too." Those in relationships need to be good listeners in order to be in tune. If you can't hear God, you may need to adjust your frequencies and theological attentiveness to the music.

Give "ear" to God.

c. Turn On to the Living Christ

If you are hearing God's voice, then you are singing your song passionately and vivaciously in the world. Once we begin to listen and tune our lives to the beauty of Christ, we take on a new step to our gait, a new rhythm to our lives. We begin to dance in step with the divine. Each day that we pray, sing, read the Scriptures of our Lord, we become more and more immersed in the rhythm of the Creator and the dance of creation.

You cannot go through the Scriptures without the Scriptures going through you. As God changes the drumbeat of our lives, we dance to a new rhythm—the rhythm of the Spirit. It's not enough to ignore the noises of culture that would seek to trip us up. We must also turn on, consciously and passionately commit ourselves to a new way of singing and dancing and being in the world. When you turn on your frequencies to the vibrations of God's Spirit, to those frequencies that announce a reality that is not yet, your heart resounds with the pulsation of the living heart of Christ.

d. Tune In to the Presence of the Spirit around You
Are you all ears?

Everywhere, all around the world, Jesus is revealing himself to his creation. Everywhere we look, we can see evidence of grace and healing. Everywhere we go, we can feel God's breath of life. Everything in the entire universe is attuned to the creating force of life. Physicists in fact tell us that the entire universe con(forms) to an "anthropic principle"—all that exists is finely tuned to a design that supports life. More so, physicists claim that certain features in the universe appear actually to be uncannily "tuned" in favor of life. For example, dark energy forms approximately 70 percent of the stuff of the known universe. This energy needs to be "tuned" to one part in ten—to the 120th power. The flamboyant atheist and Nobel Prize–winning physicist Steven Weinberg described this as "the one fine-tuning that seems to be extreme, far beyond what you could imagine just having to accept as a mere accident."[88] Sir Martin Rees has mesmerized audiences around the world with the "six universal constants" that are exquisitely attuned and without which neither our world nor life as we know it could have come into being.

In the past, theologians have been the ones struggling to see the world from a God-centered perspective. Now, even scientists are aware that our created world resonates more with mystery and the unexplained than exactitude and empirical certainty. As those who sing the Lord's song, we need to be especially attuned to the presence of the living Christ that moves freely throughout creation and within each follower of Jesus. We need to be aware of God's presence, movement, and work in the world and in all people, and we need to be continually aware that one of our voices could be the one to bring that reminder to someone in need.

Three-time Pulitzer Prize–winner Carl Sandburg got his start as a sportswriter. In 1928, when he was interviewing Babe Ruth for the

Chicago Daily News, Sandburg asked the Babe: "People come and ask what's your system for hitting home runs. That so?"

"Yes," said the Babe, "and all I can tell them is I pick a good one and sock it. Then I get back to the dugout and they ask me what it was I hit, and I tell 'em I don't know except it looked good."

The Babe had no complicated formula for hitting homers. He was in tune with the game and the home runs came.

This is no different from following Jesus. No complicated system can explain followership. But tuning yourself through love and trust can make it seem the most natural and life-giving act in the world.[89]

e. Tune Up whenever You Can

Once we are tuned in to the Spirit's frequencies, we soon discover how out of tune we are with God's rhythms and rhymes. Just as creation teems with new life, when we vibrate in tune with Christ, the Tuning Fork to the Eternal, we awaken to the resurrection promise and power of new life. The fountain of faith is the real Fountain of Youth.

From the beginning of the creation story, God is on a mission to bring humankind into intimate relationship. Through the Last Adam, we are offered life's best shot at being the authentic, real human beings our Creator originally made us to be—a return to that truly intimate, holistic, redemptive, and restorative garden relationship with God that we so yearn for from the depths of our humanness. In a sense, being in tune with God is a "walk-in-the-garden" song, a duet, an echo, a resonance of the one true Lord of Life who made us to walk in the garden. Tune-ups are garden songs ("He walks with me and He talks with me"), songs that teach us we are never alone and we can always hear God's call. The more we tune to God's Perfect Pitch, the more we will live that garden song.

For a musician, tuning is ongoing and never-ending. It isn't enough to tune only before the song, or after. Throughout the song, one must continue to pause, pay attention, retune, fine-tune, and keep attuned. Atonement is attunement.

Whether in prayer, in meditation, in singing, or in sighing, the more we pause to tune our instruments, the more creative and organic, sacred and sacramental, our voices become. Attunement recharges the soul like nothing else.

f. Resonate the Living Christ in Your Life

What's your vibe? What kind of vibe do you give off? Is Jesus your daily vibe?

Every performance is a treasury of gifts. Each musician brings to the communal chorus his or her own unique voice—and a special resonance. Vocal directors know that not only is the pitch of voice important, but each voice vibes differently. Sometimes a voice that may sound unusual by itself sounds utterly beautiful when put in combination with another or a series of others. It is collective resonance that makes for an exquisite bouquet of sound.

God's heavenly choir, like all choirs, is a blend of individual strains—each unusual and resonant in its own way. Jesus followers are devoted members of the choir. They vibe Jesus in their lives both individually and communally. The greater the body, the greater are the reverberations of God's mission and the more "surround sound" the syncopations of the Spirit—sounds that sync with every plant, every animal, every molecule of life in this world and beyond.

To resonate Christ is to birth the world into "new song," a song that can change the entire cosmos. Sometimes the world is not ready to hear the "new song." In 1913, Igor Stravinsky's thirty-three-minute *Rite of Spring* made the audience scream and shout insults. That's why

God raises up prophets and certain tribes (e.g., Issachar) who take the screams and insults until the dopamine kicks in. It takes time for the corticifugal network, those malleable cells in the auditory cortex, to learn new patterns, cut new channels, dance to new tunes, and reorganize the connections. A true "new song" ("See, I am making all things new"[90]) doesn't so much find a need and fill it as fill a need that hasn't yet been found and no one knew they had.

Resin—the stuff one puts onto the strings of a bow in order to make the sound resonate more richly—is the power of discipleship. Wesleyans fill life with the rich resin of reason, experience, Scripture, and tradition, and make joyful noises that recall the land to the triad of Truth, Beauty, and the Good.

g. Stay Tuned by Paying Attention

Seasoned musicians know that every song can be raised to the next level through transposition. When we transpose a song, we rewrite the scale patterns in another key. In a sense, we up the pitches and, in so doing, up the ante.

To stay tuned to the Spirit, we need to continually "up the pitches"— both the pitch of our commitment and the frequency of our pitch. When we live out our lives in holiness—in intentional, intensive relationship with Christ—he lifts us higher, takes us further, roots us deeper in the joy and juice of life.

But good musicianship takes constant awareness of technique and form. God can't take your life from concertino to concerto unless you are willing to practice diligently, to trust the Conductor and sing the same notes over and over again. The more you pay attention to each sign, each revealed nuance of the composition, the more beautiful the music becomes. The more you pay attention to each revealed sign of God's presence, the more beautiful your discipleship will resound in the world. Whether in your journey you encounter a time to transpose, a time to accelerate, a time to pause, a time to crescendo, a time to slow up, or a time of silence, each step in time is a unique and vital part of the music of life.

Pay attention; stay in tune. Take time to be holy.

4. DISCIPLINES OF SILENCE

A string that is always taut, breaks.
—Ancient proverb

One of my heroes is E. Stanley Jones. He is widely read and celebrated for being a Methodist missionary theologian. But I admire him for another reason: he was a great artist of stillness. Every day, seven days a week, Jones devoted the first hour to leaning on his "listening post." He stood, sat, or walked in silence and listened to the voice of God: "The LORD is in his holy temple; let all the earth keep silence before him!"[91] E. Stanley Jones mastered the art of stillness, and inspired me to sign-off letters and sign books with this triple wordplay: "Still in One Peace."

When the Bible says God "rested" on the Sabbath day, it doesn't mean God got tired and took a break. It simply means that God entered those spaces and silences without which there would be no music. Silence is God's first language, and darkness is God's home space. Humans need silence as we need food, rest, and companionship.

John Cage (1912–92) was a composer, philosopher, and poet. If people know his name at all, it is for his most famous musical composition, *Four Minutes and Thirty-three Seconds*, first performed at Woodstock, New York, in 1952. The piece consists of the pianist going to the piano and holding his hands over the keyboard without striking any keys for four minutes and thirty-three seconds.

But John Cage did not write a symphony of silence. There are three tacit movements of this piece, Cage intended to provide conceptual frames for the random noises that occurred during each one of those movements. Cage was obsessed with the noise of silence, with all that was happening in the "silences"—*between* the notes of Western music, *beyond* the notes organized by the composer. Cage turned this *between* and *beyond* into a composition that blurred the boundaries between sound and silence. "The essential meaning of silence is the giving up of intention," is how Cage redefined silence.[92] For Cage, the true distinction is not between sound and silence but between the intentionality of hearing and sounds to which you are paying attention.[93]

> *The world of "silence" is populated*
> *by a myriad of creatures and a myriad of sounds.*
> —*Rollo May*[94]

In a Muzak culture plagued with oversharing and blogorrhea, we need to learn to zip the lip. Those who speak well have first intentionally listened and listened well.

You cannot hear Jesus if you are listening to yourself (or stethoscoping your vital statistics).

You cannot see Jesus if you are looking in the mirror and worried about your appearance (or how likable or relevant you are).

You cannot touch Jesus if you are hanging on to possessions and safety nets for dear life (that includes pensions and guaranteed appointments).

You cannot taste Jesus if you are worried about the taste you are leaving in other people's mouths (or the best way to fracture the bread).

You cannot smell Jesus if you are drugged on the fumes of your ego (or love human institutions more than God).

Listening is an act of love exercising the discipline of silence. You can't hear God's applause if you never put your life on pause. The ability to pause, to obtain distance and perspective, is the essence of freedom.[95] To be schooled in spiritual rest is the opposite of being in spiritual arrest.

There is a Russian phrase, *proverka sloukha,* that is often used in telephone conversations to explain long periods of silence. It means "I have nothing special to say." Maybe if we have "nothing special to say," we should keep silence and learn the covering phrase *proverka sloukha.*

Open my ears, that I may hear
voices of truth thou sendest clear;
and while the wave notes fall on my ear,
everything false will disappear.

Silently now I wait for thee,
ready, my God, they will to see.
Open my ears, illumine me,
Spirit divine.
—*Clara H. Scott (1895)*[96]

The Greek word *catechesis* is based on our word *echo.* Catechesis literally means "echo down" or "resound." If sound does not linger and reverberate (but only dissipates), if sound doesn't remain in remembered form, then sound has not impressed itself or incarnated itself. Followership is a lifelong process of catechesis.

But there is no catechesis without silence. The first lesson for every catechumen is to learn how to "hear" or "listen." Understanding and obedience follow hearing. When the Bible talks about an "understanding heart," the real meaning is a "hearing heart." The major catechetical discipline is one of learning how to hear, how to listen, how to be quiet and be still, so that we can first hear and then obediently pass on or "echo" the person of Christ to every place and period. Catechesis is less confirmation in a body of knowledge than con-formation to the curriculum of Jesus the Christ, where every follower is a syllabus for Christ-formation.

To echo the faith means more than echoing "faith facts." Facts come and go. Facts die. Only Christ lasts. Catechesis is a lifelong process of deepening the echo of Christ that people hear in us.

5. DISCIPLINES OF BREATHING

Prayer is breath. Prayer is the breath that connects us to the God who breathed duvets of dust into "human" being. The former head of the Vatican Bank, Archbishop Paul Marcinkus, had a saying: "You can't run the Church on Hail Marys."[97] But you can run the church on "Our Fathers." You can run the church on a wing and a prayer. Jesus prayed twenty-one original prayers in the Gospels, and every one he began with "Our Father."

For Wesley, prayer was to the soul what breath was to the body. "Prayer may be said to be the breath of our spiritual life. He that lives cannot possibly cease breathing."[98] This meant that Wesleyans were proud to be known as a "praying people." Or again in Wesley's words, "A Christian prays always, at all times, and in all places, and with all sorts of prayer, public, private, mental, vocal."[99] From the very beginning, Wesleyans were known as "high-hopers," not for spray-on hope but pray-on hope.

There is a one-sentence, four-mark summary of the life of a dynamic church: "faithful to the teaching of the apostles, to the brotherhood (*koinonia*), to the breaking of bread, and to prayers."[100] A church windy with prayer is alive and spirited. A church whose prayer life winds down increases its chances of asthma attacks, with pneumonia looming on the horizon. For Wesley, prayer was the number one sign of the visible church.[101] Yes, there needed to be the proclaimed and received word. Yes, there needed to be a common sacramental life embodied in a missional community. But the most important sign of the visible church? A living, praying faith. This needs to be cemented in the cranium of every Wesleyan: a living, praying faith. Not a dead faith. A living faith empowered by prayer.

God puts life's goodies and cookies on a low shelf. You have to get on your knees to find them. Early Methodists were known for their knee-prints, just as devout Muslims are known for their prayer bumps.[102] Stories circulated widely of lifetime Methodists leaving knee-prints in the floorboards and carpets by their beds, or traveling itinerants whose bodies were found frozen in the snow, their last act of ushering their souls into eternity by prayer leaving deep knee-prints in the snow.

Where is prayer planted? More in the mind or more in the heart? There is no place in the Wesleyan world for "wordy" prayers: prayers with all the right words but none of the right feelings. The Wesley brothers didn't go so far as Martin Luther, who believed that "blasphemies, because they are violently extorted from men by the devil . . . they sometimes sound more pleasant in the ear of God than a hallelujah or some kind hymn of praise [from the pious]."[103] But for Wesleyans, you didn't so much "pray" the Lord's Prayer as you became the Lord's Prayer. Holiness was when all of life—eating, sleeping, loving, playing—was a prayer offering to God, a "Lord's Prayer." A disciple who breathed out a prayer would breathe in a blessing.[104]

*The best prayers have often more groans than words; and those
words that it hath, are but lean and shallow representation of
the heart, life and spirit of prayer.*
—*John Bunyan*[105]

There is an old German legend about a farm community that was troubled with poor harvests. Consequently, the farmers gathered together and began to pray: "Lord God Almighty, we are in desperate need of a good harvest. Therefore, we want you to promise that during the coming year, you will give us exactly what we ask for. When we ask for rain, promise us we will have rain. When we ask for sunshine, promise us we will have sunshine."

To this God agreed, according to the legend.

When the farmers asked for rain, God sent them rain. When the farmers asked for sunshine, God gave them sunshine. And the cornstalks grew tall. And the wheat grew thick. And the farmers rejoiced.

But when harvesttime came, their joy turned to sorrow because the cornstalks had produced no corn and the wheat stalks had produced no grain and the thick-leafed trees had produced no fruit.

"Lord God Almighty, you have broken your promise," the farmers cried out in dismay.

"No, my children," God replied, "I have given you exactly what you asked for."

"Why, then, do we have no kernel, and no grain, and no fruit?" the farmers asked.

God answered: "Because you did not ask for the strong north winds."

Without the winds, there was no pollination.

Without the breathings of prayer, there is no reproduction.

PRACTICE MAKES PERFECT

Austrian violinist and composer Fritz Kreisler (1875–1962) hated to practice. So he basically never did. He just performed. His wife tried to convince him to practice, but he blew her off.

After one performance, when the organizers described him as "the world's greatest musician," Kreisler turned to his wife and said, "Did you ever hear such praise?" Whereupon she said, "Just think what they would have said if you had practiced!"

> *Everything looks easy that is practiced to perfection.*
> —*Johann Wolfgang von Goethe*[106]

There are certain Greek words every Christian ought to know (e.g., *agape, metanoia, koinonia, kenosis, plerosis*). For Methodists, *ascesis* is one of them. *Ascesis* refers to the practices and disciplines of mind and body that are required for the "athletic life." *Ascesis* puts the *discipline* in *discipleship*, which is lost in the word's transliteration as "ascetic," which unfortunately has lost the "disciplined practice" connotation to mean almost exclusively extreme self-denial or self-mortification.

Every parent faces the same fateful day. Your child announces that she or he has decided to play a musical instrument. You hold your breath for what comes next, hoping your child's pick is not the tuba or drums.

Every parent of a child learning a musical instrument can tell stories of squeaks and squawks, and the same fractured tune repeated over and over again in your head.

Professional musicians, as well as the garage band guys, the Christmas party piano player, the community band enthusiasts—all seem to make their music effortlessly. But it took a lot of squeaky-squawky, off-key, eardrum-bruising moments to get to the degree of proficiency where, suddenly, they were making music.

Music that brings ecstasy and enchantment.

Music that channels creativity and sparks the imagination.

Music that fills a lonely evening.

Music that brings a party to life.

OK, OK. The hope of that mystic connection to music is why you *do* pay for that child's clarinet lessons over the summer vacation.

Most things that are worth doing take practice. They need application and tend to be enjoyable to oneself and others only once you get good at them. If the church doesn't help its members get to that point, who will?

When it sounds good, it looks easy. But it takes a lot of practice to get to that point of sounding good. Why is it we will put up with the imperfections and disruptions of "practice" when it comes to learning to play a musical instrument, but we find it so much harder to put up with the discord and dissonance that come when we are all engaged in "practicing" the greatest instrument we have each been given?

That instrument is the living Spirit of Christ within each of us.

The church is best defined as "communities of practice." A place where those who have chosen to live the life of Christ can hit flats and sharps, miss entrances, go off beat, and even get completely lost for a while—yet still be a part of the church community's "practice session" that is Christ's church. Isn't growing a soul like learning any musical instrument, a lifelong project? Yes, it brings great joy. Yes, it brings focus and direction. Yes, it brings a love of artistic perfection. But it does take continual, gradual, lifelong practice in following the Conductor.

Practice makes permanent at the same time practice makes perfect. And sometimes people are woodshedding the wrong music and following the wrong wand-wagger. We all know people who are tuning their instruments to fallacious tuning forks and fraudulent stick pickers: wealth, fame, celebrity, and hedonism. Boston College has a Center on Wealth and Philanthropy. For the past couple of years, they have been surveying 165 households with an average net worth of $78 million. These multimillionaires were asked such questions as "How would you describe the ultimate goal or deepest aspiration for your life?" Before the study, titled "The Joys and Dilemmas of Wealth," was made public, *The Atlantic* was given access to some of the reports, and a summary was written by Graeme Wood.

Are you ready for his conclusion?

If anything, the rich stare into the abyss a bit more starkly than the rest of us. The truly wealthy know that appetites for material indulgence are rarely sated. No yacht is so super, nor any wine so expensive, that it can soothe the soul or guarantee one's children won't grow up to be creeps.[107]

All the fake tuning forks can't "soothe the soul."

Then there are those who never give a single thought to their spiritual life—to "tuning" the instrument that God has implanted within them. This is not because they are "tone deaf." No one is born "tone deaf" to Truth. But they refuse to hear the dissonance between "what I want" and doing "the very thing I hate."[108] But they can't escape from how God made them: a musical instrument designed to vibrate according to the resonances of the eternal.

This is the church: an orchestra of instruments that need constant tuning. Daily, sometimes hourly, tuning. Just like any musical instrument. And it is the church that Jesus picked from the beginning to be a community where people could practice their instruments and conduct their tune-ups.

If there were ever a cast of castoffs, it was Jesus' chosen Twelve. Read the Gospels. Start with the earliest Gospel, Mark, where the disciples are the "Duh!-ciples," I call them. Do they ever get it? At one point Jesus exclaims, "How dull you are!" At another point he mutters in utter frustration, "Have I been so long time with you, and you still don't get it?"[109] There is no greater blessing to every new generation of disciples than the example of Jesus' first twelve disciples—the ones who walked with him, witnessed his miracles, and were imbued with healing powers . . . but who were slow learners and needed constant tune-ups.

Even as close to Jesus as the Twelve were, their instruments were squeaky and squawky, out of tune, and without many glimmers of harmonic grace. Mentored one-on-one by the Messiah, the Son of God, they still needed to practice.

Jesus spent his ministry on earth healing, eating, conversing, and teaching. He healed a lot of people, he taught some profound lessons, and he told some great stories. Yet his handpicked disciples didn't learn squat until after he broke out of the tomb. The disciples—the ones the church reveres as the chosen Twelve—were out-of-tune oafs while they were in the presence of God's Son. The Gospels themselves portray Jesus' disciples as fractured, fragmented, wanting to be better, but unable to meet the challenge, claim the truth, and accept the consequences. That's why they hid while he was on the cross.

The Scriptures reveal a discipleship journey from ass to apostle that is not even or straight. The grace of God is such that we can go from lost to found in a flash, from sinner to saved in a heartbeat, from bound to free in one three-letter word: *Yes!* But the discipleship story is not a simple narrative where you go from bad to good overnight, or where the good and the bad are clearly distinguished. The membrane between best and worst in each of us is very thin. If the kingdom of heaven is within us, so too is hell. The barbarians are not all outside. Mixed motives are the norm; pure self-denial the exception. We can blunder into bathos in the blink of an eye. The monster is not out there, but within, and even in the virtuous. The Messiah was killed, and ministries today are still being murdered by monsters of righteousness.

In short, the disciples are us. We are the body of Christ, but we are crippled and compromised. We want to do good. But . . . yadda, yadda, yadda . . . we do bad. But the "bad" is not what we really "want" to do.

The disciples loved Jesus. They followed him into an uncertain future. They gave up their livelihoods. They chose a life of "if" and "when" over a stable life of "here" and "now." Yet they failed to give in and give all until Pentecost gave them the spiritual infusion they needed.

Should our churches be any less patient, any less prepared for a life of practice, than that first-century community of first followers? Than Jesus himself? Methodists love to lift up people's strength and celebrate their "gifts and graces" (a phrase that's a tribal tic). At the same time, Methodists are aware of what lurks in the human heart, and thus celebrate the way God's strength is made perfect in our weakness. Maybe it's time for Methodists to require a "weakness inventory" to go along with the popular "strengths inventory."

Every Methodist must learn to "play" their life, their faith, their love. But "play" requires "practice." Playing, without apparent effort, without apparent work, is the goal. But that kind of "playing" takes a lot of practice. The church is not the concert hall for those who have got it all right. The church is the practice room for those who are working on their scales, exercising eternal études, making mistakes, getting the rhythm wrong.

The church is the place where even Paul could admit, "That was a real clambake"; that he couldn't get it all right . . . yet. But he was working on it.

If Paul could admit he hit wrong notes, and that it hadn't been the best of days for making music, can't we grant our current disciples the same "practice time" graces?

The "saints" who populate church pews are "practitioners," not "perfectionists." We are all searching for the right key, trying to keep in tune, and striving to find the melody that will resonate perfection with our ever-maturing spirit.

Can we be a community of practice?

We put up with our kids learning to play their instruments—whether it be the drums or the clarinet—because we love them. Sometimes we have to block our ears. Sometimes we have to grit our teeth. But we don't tell our kids how awful their playing is. We encourage them. We grin and bear it. Why?

Because we love them.

Do we love one another enough to be a community of practice?

CHAPTER TWO

THE SONG
OF FIRE

"Hearts Strangely Warmed":
The Power of Passion

This short book explores what it means to be, in our time, Wesleyan in general, and United Methodist in particular. Two simple gestures symbolize the genius, the defining core identity of United Methodism: relationships and passion.

Studies have shown that gestures help us think, help us learn, and help others to remember what we're learning and thinking.[1] In American Sign Language (ASL), "United Methodist" gets translated as follows: To sign "United," make circles with your thumb and middle finger of both hands. Then link the circles together, making a chain-link circle. That gesture means two persons connecting. If you make a circle in the air with your chain-linked hands, that means communities connecting. This is the ASL sign for connection, oneness, or relationships between groups.

To sign "Methodist," just rub your hands together like you are warming them by a fire or getting ready to do some work. That is the symbol for passion, or enthusiasm. John Wesley knew that the core of Jesus' ministry was about relationships and passion, and he strove to bring the world a renewed passion for Jesus, realized and lived out in everyday life. A world without passion is a world without Wesley.

There's no half-singing in the shower; you're either a rock star
or an opera diva.
—Josh Groban[2]

Methodism marked a unique articulation of the *missio dei*. The key to the Wesleyan revival of the eighteenth century was a movement connected in its mission and a movement passionate about its mission. The essence of Methodism's genius resided in these two famous Wesley mantras: "heart strangely warmed" (inward experiences with a fire in the heart); and "the world is my parish" (outward experiences with winds of kindness, mercy, and mission). For Wesley, internal combustion ("heart strangely warmed") led to external combustion ("the world is my parish").

The next chapters will explore how the uniqueness of Methodist respiration, a fiery inhalation and a windy exhalation, can be rediscovered today and redeployed as others have done in our quarter millennium of history. The keys to the twenty-first century as the "best," not "worst," of times for Wesleyans is in the ASL signing of "United Methodist," true connectionalism and passionate faith.

A Methodist by the name of William Booth founded the Salvation Army. He was addressing a rally of his troops in London one day, and he shouted out the question: "How wide is the girth of the world?" Booming back came the answer: "25,000 miles." To that Booth roared: "Then . . . we must grow till our arms get right round about it."[3]

In the eighteenth century, Methodists in general (and in their younger years, the Wesley brothers themselves) used to be accused of being too "sexy." What else could all those "love feasts" and "strangely warmed hearts" be about? Why else were all those women in positions of leadership?

We're a lot less sexy now. I have written this book in hopes of bringing back to the body some of Methodism's sexiness so that our current reproduction crisis (the greatest crisis any species can have) might be reversed. With this book, I also hope to make my case that God may have raised up John Wesley and the Methodists even more for the twenty-first century than for the eighteenth century.

The Light of the World is not starlight, light emitted from dead stars and transmitted across time that reaches us still and continues to enlighten us, but is really an echo of something long gone. God is not some Master Composer who gave us one song to sing for all eternity. The Spirit engages us in God's ongoing songs of creation, all variations on the same theme: the love of the Father for the Son. Through the resurrection presence of Jesus the Christ, the Spirit continues to sing that love song in and through us.

> *The best lack all conviction, while the worst*
> *Are full of passionate intensity.*
> —W. B. Yeats, "The Second Coming"[4]

The genius of Methodism is that it picked up and amplified the two major "sounds" that keep God's song on key and in harmony: the "sound" of wind and the "sound" of fire.

Wales has been called "a country of the heart." Methodism is a movement of the heart—but a heart that is on fire, a heart with wings beating in sync with the Spirit. Fire and wind were the two sounds that kept the early Methodist movement together and in forward motion:

1. a passion for mission and a love of God and neighbor; and

2. connectional relationships and a contagious message.

What makes a Methodist? What defines us? How can we reignite the spark of genius that motivated our ancestors in the great cloud of witnesses? How can we move our future from extinction to distinction?

Ask Methodists around the world what our greatest problems are, and you get two answers that come up again and again. We are aging, and, along with the rest of "lamestream" Protestantism, we are passionless. An old phrase refers to "those of like passions." Are we a people of passion, comprising "those of like passions"?

No heart is pure that is not passionate,
and no virtue is safe that is not enthusiastic.
— *Sir John Robert Seeley*, Ecce Homo[5]

Wesleyan spirituality means "spirited" if it means anything at all. But passion for Wesley did not mean heart-on-sleeve emotionality or giddy-kiddy love. What was labeled Methodist "enthusiasm" was really for Wesley a concentration of attention and contagion of experience that pivoted around Christ. The church is always one generalization away from extinction, and here it is "it doesn't matter what you believe."

Rembrandt was so passionate about one of his masterpieces (*The Anatomy Lesson*, I think) that he lost all track of time while working on it. One of his apprentices was fearful for his health, and challenged him: "Master, . . . you are looking drawn and tired, you are exhausted."

"No!" cried Rembrandt. "No! Spent yes, but not exhausted."[6]

For Rembrandt, *exhausted* meant "drained, empty, unfilled," but *spent* meant "fulfilled, completed, inwardly enriched and happy"! In the same way, our beauty reflects God's beauty; our passion for God reflects God's passion for us. Passion is what enabled Wesley's soul to be beefed up as his body was depleted in telling anyone who would listen that Jesus Christ alone can tell you who you are, why you're here, and where you're going.

> *A person without passion has no more value than a candle without a flame or fire without light.*
> —*Chuck Gallozzi*[7]

Has anyone ever accused you of lacking passion? Your church? The leader of the Free Church of Scotland, Thomas Chalmers (1780–1847), liked to call Methodism "Christianity in earnest."[8] For Wesley, our "earnestness" was an earnestness of eternity. The method of Methodism perfects the "pitch" or the unique voice with which we sing God's song. We can always become better singers. But no matter what the "voice," it's the "gusto," the passion, that marks Wesleyan uniqueness. The greatest historian of Christian doctrine of the twentieth century, Jaroslav Pelikan, favored this John Wesley quote to sum up the Methodist movement: "You must be singular or be damned. The way to hell has nothing singular about it, but the way to heaven is singularity all over."[9]

For some people, this "singularity" bordered on madness. It is true: noisiness could turn to nosiness. Methodists exerted themselves so passionately, so long, so tirelessly that a Quaker reportedly warned his cow who was giving him a hard time:

Thou knowest that I cannot curse thee
Thou knowest that I cannot smite thee;
But there is one thing thou knowest not:
I can sell thee to a Methodist.[10]

One of Britain's most popular poets laureate and a beloved figure on British television, Sir John Betjeman (1906–84), ranted against John Wesley's ferocity of focus in one of his radio talks. A die-hard Anglican, Betjeman resented Wesley's moral loftiness that infused with a dreadful passion not just personal choices but social vision as well:

> Where unto shall I liken Mr. John Wesley?—and with what shall I compare him? I will liken him unto a low and puny tadpole in divinity, which proudly seeks to disembowel a high and mighty whale in politics. I do not expect to be treated by Mr. Wesley with the candour of a gentleman, or the meekness of a Christian, but I wish him, for his reputation's sake, to write and act with the honesty of a heathen.[11]

Betjeman then went on to condemn Methodism for bringing to England "a narrowness of spirit, a party zeal, a being straightened in our own bowels" that issues in a "miserable bigotry."[12]

In spite of Betjeman's preference for cloaking passion in indirection and discretion, every advancement in human history has been a triumph of passion. The last gesture of a Methodist is a shrug. The last song of a Methodist is "Let Nothing You Dismay."[13] Passion is infectious, and Methodism went viral because of its no-holds-barred enthusiasm for God and the gospel. Like the nightingale, Methodists couldn't stop singing their song, even when that song went from fending off predators to attracting enemies.

John Wesley was not only passionate about faith, but passionate about life. He was always interested in the latest scientific advances, especially those that promoted wholeness of mind, body, and spirit. The promise of electrical treatments for people, new to the eighteenth century, was exciting for Wesley. So much so that he purchased an electrical machine for his own study in 1750, and the more he administered treatments to himself, the more he became convinced that electric shocks might improve people's health, especially "the passions," which was his phrase for the inward emotions. A body without "passions," Wesley believed, was a dead body, not a live one. After first introducing "electrifying" cures in *Primitive Physick* (1747), he dedicated an entire book to the subject in 1759 called *The Desideratum*, where he listed thirty-seven disorders that electrification of the body could help. He advised early Methodists: "Be electrified daily."[14]

Not bad advice for our future.

Methodism sacralized a multitude of spaces that could keep the fire burning inside: small groups (class meetings, bands, select bands), a variety of worship experiences (love feasts, quarterly meetings, annual conferences, etc.), and, beginning in the early nineteenth century, the holy hullabaloo known as the camp meeting that was the closest thing to heaven most Methodists could imagine. All these stoked the passions that kept Methodists from burnout and tended the unquenchable fire in their hearts and bellies. The soul grows only if it is nourished daily, watched patiently, and challenged periodically. But great souls are the growth of plowed soils, fallowed fields, and natural wildfires.

Passion in itself is not a virtue, however. Serial killers are passionate about their killing. When passion becomes blind rage, whether in a writer or a wrestler, it is more of a hindrance than a help. The essence of Wesleyan passion, the person and mission of Christ that we're so passionate about, can be expressed in two words: *be there*. But our passion for Christ is not a solitary expression nor a solitary mission. For Wesley, passion goes hand in hand with relationship. We are not only Methodists, but United in the love of Christ, sent out as the body of Christ into the world. When we join our passion for Christ with our passion for the Spirit of connectionalism, we add another two words: *with all*.

"*Be there*" are the passions of face and place. "*With all*" are the passions of embrace and grace. "*Be*" means we are passionate about character. "*There*" means we are passionate about context. "*With*" means we are passionate about our contacts and interrelationships. "*All*" means we are passionate about our content and our inclusiveness. "*Being there*" is keeping our "hearts warmed" in Christ. To "*be there with all*" is to celebrate the body of Christ in the world connectionally.

To "*Be there*" is to "be" the mind and heart of Christ, to embody the incarnational passion of our Lord, and to take that passion for and of Christ into the world missionally. To "*be there*" is to be passionate about our face ("Who am I? What am I here for?") and our place ("Where am I? What is to be done?"). To "*be there*" is to get our act together and to get other people together: to know Christ and to make Christ known.[15]

BE

For Aristotle, wisdom was the knowledge of being. For followers of Jesus, wisdom is the "be-ing" of Christ. By grace through faith, we have been given an existing power to "be Jesus" (a little-j) in the world. Like an elastic band with the capacity to stretch, we choose whether or not to exercise that existing power. But being in capacity a little-j has being a Big-J as part of the human essence.

Be is the character word. We must rediscover our passion about living the identity of Christ. For Wesley, discipleship formation came about not through learning content or implementing programs, but through a process of becoming j-people. Formation was not a process of confirmation and information, but con-formation and in-formation.

Charles Wesley, John Wesley, and their sister Kezia all had religious experiences the same week of May 1738. We know of John's phrase for his conversion that came on May 24, 1738, while listening to Luther's *Preface to Romans*: "I felt my heart strangely warmed. I felt I did trust in Christ, Christ alone, for my salvation."[16] But what of Charles's phrase?

Charles—a better preacher than John, the one who started the Holy Club at Oxford, the one whose hymns are sung on Sundays and never a John sermon preached—said three days before his brother John's famous experience of feeling his heart "strangely warmed" that he felt a "strange palpitation of heart" that left him "at peace with God and rejoicing in the hope of Christ."[17] Peace, joy, and hope were no longer holy abstractions, but the holy incarnate, the mystery taking bodily form and becoming sacramental.

The experiences of two German immigrants to the United States, less known but still important to the United Methodist heritage: Philip William Otterbein (United Brethren Church) and Jacob Albright (Evangelical Church), are worth noting. In 1754 Otterbein had a critical experience in his spiritual life similar to that of John and Charles. After being questioned about the meaning of grace—he had just preached a sermon on "God's Grace"—he "went into a quiet room where after fervent prayer he suddenly experienced the inner assurance of God's grace. His preaching, which had been fervent before, now became much more confident and convincing. His preaching was given in the form of direct witness to the people."[18] Albright's spiritual awakening came sometime around 1795. In his words, "One joyful experience followed another, and such a heavenly joy pervaded my whole being, as no pen can describe and no mortal can express. . . . My prayers were no longer mere entreaties but praise and hearty thanksgiving were also brought as an offering, mingled with tears of joy, to the giver of every good gift."[19]

What made the "strange" in Charles Wesley's "strange palpitation of heart," in John Wesley's "strangely warmed heart," Otterbein's "inner assurance," and Albright's "joyful experiences"?

Their hearts came alive to the mystery of Christ.

There is a little tale called "Stone Deaf." Here it is in poetic form:

> I used to be stone deaf. I would
> see people stand up and go through
> all sorts of gyrations. They called
> it dancing. It looked absurd to me
> —until one day I heard the music.[20]

On different days of the same week, the ears of three Wesleys were opened to the music being played by God in their lives. Their hearts came alive . . . and the world has never been the same since.

Hearing the music for themselves did not come easily to the Wesleys. Willliam Briggs wrote a rather amazing letter to John Wesley about the dangers of an Enlightenment faith on April 5, 1750, when Wesley was twenty-eight years of age. Briggs was Wesley's book steward from 1753 to 1759. He also helped Grace Murray when she was depressed in 1744. Briggs complained to rationalist, Oxford don Wesley:

> You have the *knowledge* of all *experience*, but not the *experience* of all you *know*. You *know* . . . the beginning and end of *true religion*. . . . I think your *experience* is *buried* in your extensive *knowledge*. I think you *feel not abidingly* a deep sense of your own spiritual *weakness*, the *nearness* of Christ to save, or a *sweet communion* with God by the Holy Ghost. You have the *appearance* of all Christian graces, but they do not, I think, spring from a *deep experience* or change of *nature*.[21]

John Wesley's father's dying words had haunted him: "The inward witness, son, the inward witness that is the proof, the strongest proof of Christianity." So too had Moravian bishop Gottlieb Spangenberg's challenge to Wesley after he arrived in Georgia: "Do you know yourself? Do you know Jesus Christ?"

Wesley replied, "I know He is the Savior of the world."

"True, but do you know He has saved you?"

"I hope He has died to save me." Wesley squirmed.

Spangenberg wouldn't let Wesley off the hook: "Do you know yourself?"

"I do."

Wesley lied.[22]

---

*To have continually before their Eys the sentence of God's
Predestination, is a most dangerous Downfall, wherby
the Devil doth thrust [Curious and Carnal Persons] into
Desperation. . . . [Satan] cannot endure that we should believe
that God is Love.*
—*Thomas Traherne (1636–74)*[23]

It was one thing to say that "God is love." Wesley deemed these three words the most important description of God in the whole Bible. But it is another thing to move from "God is love" to "God loves me." The former is an intellectual grasp; the latter is an experiential grip. It was this same know-for-yourself experience that marked Charles Wesley's conversion, except in Charles's case he was reading Luther's *Commentary on Galatians* and learned to apply these words "so dearly beloved of the Son of God, that he gave himself for me" to himself.[24]

Both John and Charles added experience to the classical Anglican triad of Scripture, reason, and tradition, signaling a profound shift away from a purely dogmatic or doctrinal definition of the Christian witness toward something more spiritual, more relational, more attitudinal: a Wesleyan way of living the resurrection life of Christ. When any religious tradition shrinks into a dogmatic system, whether the "dogmas" be theological correctness or political correctness, the dry bones rattle in one's ears and hollow out the soul.

Experience may be Methodism's cardinal rule of faith and order. But the word *experience* has a referent: it is experience of Christ, the religious experience of redemption, not "experience" in terms of "life experience" or "emotions." A full human life requires experience *as* an experience *of* where God is discovered and experienced in the ordinariness of life; not only in "holy" rites and rituals but in mundane, human tasks and daily experiences where Christ is already present.

Charles Wesley's passion for Christ is reflected in how many of his hymns begin with the word *Jesus* or *Christ*. John Wesley's passion for Christ is reflected in how many of his sermons focus on some aspect of Jesus' life, death, resurrection, and return. For John and Charles, the four Gospels were Jesus biographies, not doctrinal treatises. The passion of early Methodism was the passion of the early church: "And he brought him to Jesus."

The only passion that gives us life and not death is a passion for Jesus. A "United Methodist" usually lacks at least one of two things: either the "United" or the "Methodist." What brings the two together, the link joining the two, is our center of narrative gravity: a passion for Jesus the Christ. All things cohere in him. We are unable to make our existence cohere, to pull our lives together, without him.

There is an old Methodist hymn that captures the passion and wonder we once were lost in but now have left behind and must get lost in once again:

> Whate'er I say or do,
> . . . .
> Jesus, my single eye
> Be fix'd on thee alone;
> Thy name be praised on earth, on high,
> Thy will by all be done.

Spirit of Faith, inspire
My consecrated heart;
Fill me with pure, celestial fire,
With all thou hast and art.[25]

We now have lots of passions—justice, love, peace, simplicity. But our greatest passion is Jesus. Mennonite theologian Myron S. Augsburger, former president of Eastern Mennonite College and Seminary, gave this as his personal credo:

> I believe in justice,
>> but I am not a preacher of the gospel of justice,
>> but the Gospel of Christ who calls us to justice.
> I believe in love,
>> but I am not a preacher of the gospel of love,
>> but the Gospel of Christ who calls us to love.
> I am committed to peace,
>> but I am not a preacher of the gospel of peace,
>> but the Gospel of Christ who calls us to peace.
> I believe in the value of the simple life,
>> but I am not the preacher of the simple life,
>> but of the Gospel of Christ that calls us to the simple life.

Augsburger concluded with this warning: "Let us beware of the ultimate plagiarism of borrowing some great concepts from Jesus, then running off proclaiming these concepts and not sharing the Christ that empowers these concepts."[26]

If a movement is not moving,
it's a monument, not a movement.
—Evangelist James O. Davis

THERE

There is the context word. We are passionate about "be-ing" Christ in the context in which we find ourselves.

In every Wesleyan hymnbook with a title index, the first song listed is always the same. It is a context song: "A Charge to Keep I Have." In the second stanza Charles Wesley defines the nature of that charge— "To serve the present age / my calling to fulfill." But the life-and-death seriousness by which we are "called" to "serve" the moment God has given us—not a moment we wish we had, not a moment for which we feel more prepared, but the moment we find ourselves in by the providence and sovereignty of God—is evident in every single stanza:

1. A charge to keep I have,
   a God to glorify,
   a never-dying soul to save,
   and fit it for the sky.

2. To serve the present age,
   my calling to fulfill;
   O may it all my powers engage
   to do my Master's will!

3. Arm me with jealous care,
   as in thy sight to live,
   and oh, thy servant, Lord,
   prepare a strict account to give!

4. Help me to watch and pray,
   and on thyself rely,
   assured, if I my trust betray,
   I shall forever die.[27]

Early Methodist preachers liked to talk about a gospel "for every time and clime." "Time" and "clime" were different, although the same incarnational strategy of cultural engagement applied to both: be "in" the culture but not "of" the culture—but not "out of it" either.[28]

"Time" meant "moment of time." One of my favorite cultural exercises is to look around at every church I worship in, and ask this question: "What year is it here?" By and large, the Wesleyan tribe is filled with Gutenberg churches in a Google world.[29] We have been left stranded and gawking by the surprising changes of the past twenty years, preferring the security of the past to the romance of the future. Rather than face mind-blowing realities, we fondle and coddle head-shrinking fictions about the new world we find ourselves in.

I will never forget opening a book written less than five years ago by a bishop, where on the very first page of the preface of the book, he thanks a friend for her gift of "typing tirelessly" and "ordering" the author's "note cards." There is a vast difference between doing church in a time capsule and being the body of Christ Prime Time.

Clime meant diverse tempers or seasons within that moment of time. A church living its time doesn't necessarily live its clime. The program-based or franchise model of doing church reflects a church in its time but is a church out of clime. In this TGIF culture (Twitter-Google-iPhone-Facebook), how many Gutenbergers are like the teary kindergartner on the first day of school: "You aren't home-sick already, are you?" the teacher asked. "No, I'm *here* sick."

Life is an affair of people and place. Jesus cried over both. Once he cried over a person—the death of his best friend Lazarus (every pastor should reflect on the fact that Jesus' "best friend" wasn't one of his disciples). Once he cried over a place—the city he loved. Jesus loved a zip code enough to cry over it.

Do we love our zip code enough to cry over it? Do we even know our zip code enough to cry over it? Do we know our zip codes enough to know where their best hangouts and front porches are?[30]

Though this call did not seem to me to be in conflict with God and his Word, yet I argued, I am an uneducated and very ordinary man; how many persons of great gifts and learning there are, who would be much better instruments than I am, persons who would make a better impression.
—Jacob Albright[31]

Some of Jesus' last words to us were these: "Go into all the world and preach the gospel to every creature." If our field is the world, does this not make us all *world* missionaries? Didn't Wesley say "the world is my parish"?

Not so fast on that "world" front. Yes, the "Great Commission" is a global charge. And we are called to be "global missionaries," even "global citizens of planet Earth," as some are calling it. But we must not get there too soon. We can be so "global" that we can't see across the street. Or as the rap on academia has it, we can love everybody in general so much that we love nobody in particular very much.

One of my favorite humorists was George Carlin. But I was never sure whether Carlin loved the humans he made such fun of. In fact, one of the easiest ways of loving people is to avoid their company.

Or at least avoid crossing the street. Methodists have always read Jesus' last words as a call to be what Rick Shrout delightfully and mischievously calls "street-crossers."[32] We all need to begin our "world mission" somewhere. So why not start simply and locally? The glory of the local church is that it's global. But the only way to the global is through the local. The only way to the universal is through the provincial, a particular location or an allegiance. Before the world can be our parish, the parish must be our world—and that last phrase must be heard as positive, not negative (as long as it comes joined at the hip with the first). Is our view of the world one of vast organizations, global networks, and multinational corporations? Or is it one of small communities with idiosyncratic splashes of local color, little locales loved large with large love?

Wesley's renewal movement started in his homeland. You can't cross life's Rubicons until you first cross the street. Can we "cross" the street where we live? Can we redeem the phrase "Don't cross me!" to "You crossed me"?

America's greatest living poet, Wendell Berry, who was "locavore" before the word was cool, warns that "applied religion, without a local orientation and a local practice, can be as irresponsible, as dangerous, and as sloppy as modern science similarly applied."[33] Of course, you don't go to the other extreme and love only the particular at the expense of the universal. Clergyman Jonathan Swift wrote in November 1725 to Alexander Pope a famous letter. On the eve of the publication of his classic satire on human nature called *Gulliver's Travels* (1726), Swift asked his friend to do him a favor:

> When you think of the world give it one lash the more at my request. I have ever hated all nations, professions, and communities, and all my love is towards individuals: for instance, I hate the tribe of lawyers, but I love Counsellor Such-a-one and Judge Such-a-one. . . . But principally I hate and detest that animal called man, although I heartily love John, Peter, Thomas, and so forth. This is the system upon which I have governed myself many years, but do not tell.[34]

Hungarian novelist and antitotalitarian crusader Arthur Koestler built his antitotalitarian crusades on his opposition to dissolving the single person into the hive mentality of the community. He refused to believe that the individual "is the result of a crowd of a million divided by a million." At one point Koestler even confessed, "I don't believe any more in humanity. I believe in the individual."[35]

For Methodism, the universal is found first in the vulgar vernacular. We are all writing the stories of our lives from common plotlines of feelings, experiences, and thoughts while each person adds a unique twist that makes his or her suite of stories uniquely personal. Shrout says it best:

> To be a follower of Jesus, to be his disciple, is to be on a mission. It is to be a missionary to the other side. Street crossers are people who "cross" the street for the sake of Christ and the world. In their going—in their "crossing" of the street—they make the sign of the cross by becoming a bridge from one world to another. That crossing is both sacrificial and sacramental.[36]

What recent Methodism has sometimes forgotten is to make sure that when you "cross over" to the other side, you still take the cross over.

To be "there" is to rejoice in the particular, to crisscross the streets of our zip code. In our centralized, routinized, rationalized, rule-oriented, bureaucratic mind-set, where "order" now means juridical order instead of missional order, we can be about as uncomprehending of our local culture as the newspaper ad that read "Illiterate? Write now for free advice." Baptist missiologist Ed Stetzer once heard a veteran missions professor at a Southern Baptist seminary tell this jabbing joke: "How do you start a new Southern Baptist church in a big city up north? That's easy. You go into local grocery stores and introduce yourself to all of the people who buy grits."

The point, of course, is that this is what you do *not* want to do. But we do it all the time. It's easier to replicate than reproduce: to replicate a mass-produced program than to reproduce an original by intimate investigation of and investment in one's home ground—its seasons, flora, fauna, smells, sounds. We'd rather colonize the local than parent local color.

I'm a cheese addict, in spite of the fact that I grew up on government cheese. Dairy foods were once looked down on as principally the food of the poor, but that food of the poor has now become an artisan food that can command higher prices per pound than prime rib or lobster. My first trip to Switzerland was capped off by a visit to the home of my favorite artisanal cheese: Appenzeller. Few things make the Swiss angrier than what we have done with their festive cheeses. Technically, there is no such thing as "Swiss cheese." Putting holes in some flat white cheese and calling it "Swiss" is like mass-producing bricks out of bland yellow cheese and calling it "Velveeta." Switzerland is dotted with villages that make artisanal cheeses, each one handcrafted in small batches, and made with the highest-quality ingredients to create tastes that can be savored and identified by their local flair and flavor.

> *The universal must be local to be real.*
> *— An ecumenical necessity*[37]

In late 2011 Domino's Pizza launched an "artisan pizza." Maybe it's time the church launched some "artisan churches." Indeed, churches of the future must have an artisanal quality, just as apostolic churches did. The only differences in the churches named in the Scriptures were the differences of locality. There was one church in one place known by its geographic placement (Rome, Ephesus, Thessalonika, Philippi, etc.).[38] Wesley kept this principle in place with his basic organizational unit of Methodism at the community level called the "society," which consisted of all the Methodists who lived in a specific geographical area.

Artisan communities are the ultimate expression of "thereness"—God-made, homespun communities practicing humanity as God's artwork with heart-wings for the world. The more Facebook the culture, the more face-to-face, in-your-face, God's-face are our hungers and desires. The more lifelike the substitute, the more we are reminded that it is not the original. Social media are bringing in their wake a huge revival and return to shared life together. Whether our churches can be relationally authentic enough to participate in such a revival is the only question.[39]

But at the same time we are part of our zip code, we are at odds with it. We are not called to "give the good word," an old Irish expression that means telling people what they want to hear, or giving the answer that people want you to give them. We are called to "give the good news," which can be "bad" before it is "good." The socially disruptive power of the gospel is in its insistence on an alternative stance and slant. We are "in" but not "of" (nor "out of") our time and clime.[40]

So what is the best thing you can do for your zip code? Sing your own song. God needs you to be you, not to meet someone's needs or sing a song that is "relevant" to your context. God put you in a zip code. Find out your true song, your "new song"[41] in that context. Discover the relevance of irrelevance. Jesus promised to make not all things "relevant," but all things "new." Don't do what people expect you to do. Do, like Jacob Albright, what you feel inside God is calling you to do.[42] And if you're really listening to God, you'll do what that zip code needs, because that's why God put you there.

When you practice your passion for Jesus, you will "be there."

CHAPTER THREE

THE SONG OF WIND

"Life in the Spirit": The Power of Connection

Wesleyans are a "connectional" people, but the connection has increasingly become connective to structure and bureaucracies and programs and less to people and mission and places. We have even come to the point where we believe that the deeper into political action you are (whether of the right or the left), the deeper into discipleship you are going.

Unus homo, nullus homo.
Man alone is no man at all.
—Roman slogan

For Wesley, and for Otterbein and Albright, it is not enough to be passionate about your faith. To *be* in a Wesleyan Way, and especially to be United Methodist, is to be passionate about the way your faith connects with others, embraces others, includes others, loves others.

WITH

With is the contact word, the embrace of grace. We are passionate about the contacts and connections that constitute a person. A person is *never* a solo individual. A person is *always* a web of "withs," a network of relationships with ramifications that ripple out into the world. Methodism's trinitarian concept of God is by definition relational. The primacy of relations in both the divine and the human is the prized heirloom of our family silver.

Estranged is the opposite of a "strangely warmed" heart. Jesus can only live in *my* life if he lives in *our* lives, since it is the Holy— "midst"[1]—Spirit who empowers Christ's body and enables it to be holy. Have we made religion a hand-folding, hand-clapping, hand-wringing affair when it was meant to be a hand-holding, handoff, hand-up affair? There are times in my life when I hold on to you, while you hold on to Jesus. For various reasons I can't hold on to Jesus myself, but I can hold to you. Then I feel his hold on me through you, since he never lets go of either of us.

When Wesley insisted that God's grace should be experienced, he called this the "witness of the Spirit." But when he talked about how to experience the "witness of the Spirit," he talked about radial relationships and intermedial interstices: joining a class, going to church, taking the Lord's Supper, visiting the sick, participating in the "social graces," and so forth. In other words, the "witness of the Spirit" is a relational witness, a "midst" presence "where two or three are gathered together"—not exclusively, to be sure, but primarily and most definitively and ordinarily ("ordinary grace") while allowing for the possibility of "extraordinary grace" (the direct, unmediated still small voice).

For Methodism, "holy conferencing" is a means of grace. There is a dialogue of words. But there is an even more powerful dialogue of life—living together in community, sharing life together, facing common daily problems together, and being accountable to one another. The Wesleyan Way made "withness" into an art form: trial bands, select bands, class meetings, quarterly meetings; then a communion of communities known as societies, conferences, camp meetings, love feasts—practices adopted by both Otterbein and Albright at the onset of their ministries.[2] At its best, Wesleyan worship is the witness of withness, not the other way around. When the grammar of God moves from the relational language of witness and worship to the descriptive language of absolute determinative propositions, we have moved away from Methodist heritage to Methodist heresy.

To save a species, including our own, you need to preserve its entire habitat. No one understood the dangers of a singleton society better than Wesley, who outlined multiple habitations of holiness where spiritual practices could take place in a context of layered accountability. The accountability involved in all this "withness" has led some high-strung historians to argue rather hysterically that Methodist pietism was the beginning of the modern "police state," as it encouraged neighbors to "rat" on one another.[3] Others critiqued Methodism for its pietistic devotional intimacy, even Catholic tendencies. Josiah Conder, editor of the influential *Congregational Hymn Book* of 1836, described Wesley's more personal and devotional hymns as "monastic, feminine and mawkish" and "smacking of the devotion of the Roman mystic."[4] The truth is that for early Methodists, intimacy was the gift, not the goal, of relationships.[5]

There are no islands anymore.
—Edna St. Vincent Millay[6]

A Texas Lutheran men's group went up to St. Louis to cook a barbecue for the seminarians at Concordia Seminary. The men from Texas were in the kitchen cutting fat off the meat. One of the seminarians asked why they didn't just cook it with the fat on and let the seminarians cut off their own fat. One of the Texans grabbed the young man by the arm and took him outside. He told the young man to stop and reflect for a minute on what he heard while the men were cutting the fat off the meat. The young seminarian thought for a minute, and said he remembered hearing the men talking, joking, and swapping stories. The Texan then said, "That is why we cut the fat off the meat."

We need to continue to create places of "withness" hospitable to conversations and hearing one another's stories. Maybe two of the most holy places in the church building are the hallways and fellowship halls.[7]

Historians have demonstrated that the religious establishment's dispute with Jesus over Jewish law was less about belief and more about bureaucratic rectitude, about whether Jesus would maintain allegiance not to the Torah but to the synagogue community and its rules.[8] The greatest indictment against all organized religion and every bureaucracy are these accusatory words leveled against Jesus in the Temple: "This man receives sinners still."[9] Jesus answered this attack with three short stories—the lost coin, the lost sheep, the lost son—the last of which stands as the greatest short story ever told. But the very fact that these words—"This man receives sinners still"—could ever be uttered as an accusation when they are, in truth, the only hope of the world and the only hope for every one of us, shows how the church suffocates itself with the cretinisms of bureaucracies, especially St. Robert's Rules of Order instead of St. Paul's Rules of the Spirit.

Pythagoras' theorem can be stated in 24 words. The Lord's Prayer [in] 70 words. The Ten Commandments [in] 179 words. But the millennium edition of The Constitutional Practice and Discipline of the Methodist Church *required no less than 225,966 words —to tell us what?*
—Angela Shier-Jones[10]

The transition from "command-and-control" hierarchies to "connect-and-collaborate" networks is going full steam in almost every sector of society with the notable exception of the church. In the culture, "the consumer is in control." In the church, distribution hierarchies or clerical elites are in control. The greatest buzzword in organizational development is "user-generated content." In this time of flux when everything seems up for grabs, the one thing everyone agrees on is this: the people must be in control. Some are calling it "pro-am" (as in professional-amateur). But whatever you call it, there is a new standard of excellence: it is no longer the quality of the performance, but the quality of the participation.

One of the most revolutionary features of the Wesleyan revival was its liberation of the laity for leadership, and its blurring of the lines between clergy and lay when it came to priestly functions and spiritual guides. Wesley didn't worry about qualifications since he trusted on-the-job training and expected all Methodists to be lifelong learners. Growth in theological depth and priestly skills was what it meant to be Methodist.

It is not Wesleyan to give liturgy over to the liturgists, or preaching to the preacher. In fact, in early Methodism, every sermon was a tag-team match, with the itinerant delivering the formal exegesis of the sermon, but the local "exhorter" bringing the sermon home and inviting people to the altar. The function of the ministers and the itinerants is to be the *pastor pastorum* (PP)—shepherd of the shepherds, those responsible for the schooling of the shepherds. We have reduced clergy to social workers instead of pastors, and motivational speakers instead of preachers, and marketers instead of evangelists, and "cultural architects" instead of priests, and leaders instead of prophets.

No denomination has a future that does not transition from regulation to resource (with accountability), from "command-and-control" to "connect-and-collaborate." Regulation is the religious equivalent of cement shoes. In fact, eleven charges of the twelve-count indictment against John Wesley that led to his escape from Georgia under cover of darkness were ecclesiastical charges like this third one: Wesley introduced into worship musical compositions not inspected or authorized by any proper judicature.

When you centralize decision making toward a single outcome, or strive for control and consensus, you move further away from both. Shift toward making relationships, building connections, and encouraging the creativity of critical mass, and you work toward collaborative solutions. If we relinquish hierarchical control to the grass roots, and build a climate of experimentation that supports innovation, those who love the church the most will have the best ideas and will innovate the best. Some things will fail.

But Jesus gave us a sacrament of failure that frees us to fail. Planning cycles and strategic plans are killing us. Maybe it's time to place some bets and prophesy our way forward.

> *People today simply aren't willing to support*
> *an institution whose sole reason for existence*
> *is the maintenance of the institution.*
> —*Andrew C. Thompson*[11]

ALL

At a fashionable fund-raiser, Sir Wilfred Grenfell was asked by a patron, "Do you mean to tell me, Dr. Grenfell, that you are a missionary?" His reply was, "Do you mean to tell me, madam, that you are *not*?"[12]

In Methodism, the burden of proof is on the disciple of Jesus who is NOT in mission. Jesus breathed on his disciples a mission: "As the

Father has sent me, even so I send you."[13] The commissioning word is *all*: "Go into *all* the world and preach the gospel to *all* creation."[14] If the field is the world, does this not make us all world missionaries? Besides, the church can no longer afford the elitism of an earlier cultural moment when a sizable constituency of initiates could be assumed. You don't become "all things to all people" to become like them. You become "all things to all people" to woo them to Christ.

If the only way open to us for the knowledge of God were solely that of the reason, the human race would remain in the blackest shadows of ignorance.
—*Thomas Aquinas*, Summa Contra Gentiles, 4.4[15]

For Wesley, missiology was the opposite of misology. Methodism is a tradition that plumps for reason. For Wesley, the search for truth gives an intellectual richness to life. Wesley's intellectual appetites were ravenous, but he channeled these appetites into missiological directions. We want every need met, every want fulfilled, every desire matched, every hunger quenched, and every thirst satisfied, except the "hunger and thirst after righteousness." William Law, whose *A Serious Call to a Devout and Holy Life* (1728) was profoundly influenced by John and Charles Wesley, wrote to John: "The head can as easily amuse itself with a living and justifying faith in the blood of Jesus, as with any other notion."[16]

The Enlightenment thirst for knowledge, and its search for a new intellectual direction for Western culture, featured a God who was seen as a rational being. Indeed, one of the main things that makes God *God* is the mind. The Enlightenment expressed this notion in a variety of ways, but one of the most poignant was after Dr. Samuel Johnson had a paralytic stroke. Living in fear that he might lose his mind as well as his motion, he wrote a touching little collect in four Latin elegiac lines:

Father Supreme, whatever be Thy care
Touching this body (Jesu, plead the prayer),
Spare me my mind, nor count it fault in me
If that I ask which most pertains to Thee.[17]

But Wesley departed from the Enlightenment rationalist paradigm in significant ways. He never isolated reason from imagination, emotion, and liturgy. He did not think that apologetics required a rationalist project of proofs. As interested in science as he was, Wesley believed scientific explanations explain everything and nothing. Is knowledge of God primarily accessible through discursive reasoning? Or is knowledge of God accessible through personal knowledge, less captured in formulas and propositions than in narratives and metaphors (which I call narraphors), with narraphoric loops, flows, and oxbows often flooding out to fertilize unfamiliar plains? Hegel's dictum "God does not offer himself for observation"[18] does not mean that we can't "know God," but that God can't be picked up with tweezers for dissection in a pan.[19] We must accept our creaturehood. How did Nicholas of Cusa put it? We are all "doctors of ignorance." We must bear our restraints, wear our finitude. The more we take on the humility of humanity, the more freedom we enjoy.

For Wesley, a rational turn of mind was congruent with a moral turn of mind was congruent with a liturgical turn of mind was congruent with a charismatic turn of mind. When someone objected to John Wesley that too much importance was being attached to charismatic phenomenon and ecstatic experiences, he suggested that the danger might be that we pay too little attention to them.[20] Like Martin Luther, Wesley rejected a philosophical grounding for Christian faith, because he knew as an Oxford don that reason can be dragooned to prove almost anything, including (most recently) the rational possibility of dragons and zombies.[21] But conversation and deliberation were deemed better routes to rationality than introspection and meditation; and in the marketplace of ideas, Methodists have always believed that the more rationally strong ones will survive, and the more frivolous ones will shrivel and die. The life of Christ is a daily boxing ring where the head and the heart, faith and reason, doubt and certainty, duke it out by day, and then sleep together at night.

> *The Enlightenment was a movement in which the striving for truth was more important than its acquisition.*
> —Historian Stephen Bronner[22]

All is a loaded word in Wesleyan theology.

Our "allness" has become know-it-allness. We are now the resident know-it-alls. We have to have an opinion on everything, and publish a book of know-it-allness called the *Book of Resolutions*, which gets bigger every year. Our narcissism thinks that anybody cares about these tribal exercises that get us so worked up. But every time I want to get on my tribe about its know-it-allness, I remind myself of the Catholic Church's five-hundred-page *Compendium of the Social Doctrine of the Church*.[23]

First, "Four Alls" were the memorable summing-up of Methodist doctrine:

1. All need to be saved.
2. All can be saved.
3. All can know that they are saved.
4. All may be saved to the uttermost.[24]

It's that last one that is the hardest to understand today. Yet should it be?

On the final pages of Charles Darwin's *On the Origin of Species*, there is this affirmation: "And as natural selection works solely by and for the good of each being, all corporeal and mental endowments will tend to progress towards perfection."[25] Why is it people can handle a Darwinian optimism about the ways of nature better than they can a Wesleyan optimism about the ways of God? Why is it that people can want the "perfect wedding," the "perfect marriage," the "perfect kitchen," or the "perfect garden," and then be satisfied with an "imperfect spirit" or an "imperfect love"? When the Bible says we are created in the image of God, for Wesley it refers as much to our destiny as to our pedigree.

Second, "allness" was key to liturgy. Wesley said that communion was a "converting" ordinance. Communion was less one of "All who love the Lord Jesus Christ come forward," and more one of "All whom the Lord Jesus loves come forward."

Third, "allness" means a holistic faith that "unite[s] the pair so long disjoined, knowledge and vital piety; learning and holiness combined, and truth and love let all men see."[26] John Wesley represented the Enlightenment at its best. He showcased the three fundamental principles of the Enlightenment—tolerance, reason, and humanity—while never separating or stratifying the left brain and right brain, or the reach for reason from the leap of faith. For Wesley, a sermon had no right to call itself such that left the hearer either intellectually or emotionally untouched.

In what were for Wesley two separate works of God in the soul, justifying and sanctifying grace, Wesley brought the Protestant Reformed traditions and Catholic tradition together. Justifying grace set the disciple free from the guilt of sin. Sanctifying grace set the disciple free from the power of sin. In the former, you saw the Reformation's "justification by grace through faith." In the latter, you saw the "Catholic" understanding of works as a continuing "means of grace."

The legal minds, the devoutly religious, want Jesus to draw a line in the sand and name who is my "neighbor" and who is not. After all, we can't be responsible for everyone.

Jesus refuses. Jesus doesn't draw a line; he draws a picture and tells the story of a despised Samaritan who stumbles on a half-dead crime victim after a priest and a Levite have passed him by. The Samaritan binds his wounds, picks him up, and carries him to the nearest inn where he arranges to cover his care and healing. Jesus then answers the lawyer's question with a question of his own: Who was a neighbor? The one who had mercy on him.[27] By telling us to "go and do likewise," Jesus is asking us not to go on a hunt for the wounded, but to be a neighbor to everyone we meet, even if he is a Samaritan. A neighboring relationship with the needy is the true definition of the church—an agape network that reaches out to all, especially the stranger and the estranged.

For Jesus, the front lines were the fault lines. It is *SO GOD* for the Spirit to be found most profoundly in the most godforsaken places.

The Spirit breaks out ecstatically. You can't control it. Unlike the waves of the sea, which live by "thus far and no further," the waves of the spirit blow where they will.

Has the wind gone out of our sails?

And through all sound of gaiety and quest [we]
Have heard a kitten in the wilderness.
—Hart Crane, "Chaplinesque"[28]

Love has shown itself in our midst as the particular universal; ethical passages and moral pasturage have found their content in a human personage: Jesus of Nazareth. Not only whoever sees him sees the Father;[29] but whoever loves another, loves him in the person of that other.[30] In the theology of Jesus, outside the Holy Spirit, the third person of the Trinity, there are no third persons. Only first and second persons.

When the Wesleys arrived on the scene, English society was in the pits of misery and degradation. Fifty-five percent of children died before age five. There was one alehouse for every twenty households. London was the sex capital of the world, like Amsterdam and Bangkok today. Throughout the eighteenth century, London had more prostitutes per capita than any other European city. Best estimates are 50,000 prostitutes for a male population of about 350,000. Even if there were only half that, that's still a lot with almost nobody being arrested, nobody convicted, and open solicitation. When Wesley came on the scene, Baron de Montesquieu (1689–1755) said, "There is no religion in England. If anyone mentions religion people begin to laugh."[31] Poverty was much the same when the first celebrity novelist, Jack London, described a London scene a hundred years after Wesley: "From the slimy sidewalk, they [the poor and homeless] were picking up bits of orange peel, apple skins and grape stems, and they were eating them."[32]

It is to these Samaritans, those who live outside the palladium of property and privilege, that the Methodist mission is directed. Life is already in the condition of the "spiritual." Life is the arena of the Spirit. To go deeper into life is to go deeper into the life of the Spirit. Miss J. C. March wrote to John Wesley and asked how best to mature her faith. John answered with an elaboration of prevenient grace: "Go see the poor and sick in their own poor little hovels. Take up your cross, woman! . . . Jesus went before you, and will go with you. Put off the gentlewoman; you bear a higher character. You are an heir of God!"[33] When Jesus is Lord, our lords become the poor, the sick, the hungry, the hurting.

It is the LORD who goes before you.
—*Deuteronomy 31:8*

Wesley worked against electoral corruption; structured systematic distribution of food, medicine, clothing, loans, and money; and organized temporary employment to the destitute. For Wesley, "works of piety" and "works of mercy" constituted the heart of holiness. In his sermon "On Zeal," he argued that "works of mercy" take precedence over "works of piety." Or in his exact words, "Whenever, therefore, one interferes with the other, works of mercy are to be preferred. Even reading, hearing, prayer, are to be omitted, or to be postponed, 'at charity's almighty call'—when we are called to relieve the distress of our neighbor, whether in body or soul."[34]

Paul asks, "Do you want to reach maturity?" The Greek word for "maturity" is the same word for "perfection." But we need to put "Be perfect as your Father is perfect" in context. Here it is:

> You have heard that it was said, "You shall love your neighbor and hate your enemy." But I say to you, Love your enemies and pray for those who persecute you. . . . For if you love those who love you, what reward do you have? Do not even the tax collectors do the same? And if you greet only your brothers and sisters, what more are you doing than others? Do not even the Gentiles do the same? Be perfect, therefore, as your heavenly Father is perfect.[35]

Jesus defines perfection in terms of lush love and plush hospitality.

In "charity," as in so much else, there is an identifiably Methodist way of doing things. Methodists create a style out of plainness and wholeheartedness. Many Calvinists think you get into heaven headfirst. Many Catholics think you get into heaven feetfirst. Methodists said you get into heaven heartfirst. Instead of wearing their hearts on their sleeves, Methodists wore their hearts in their heads, and they especially wore their hearts in their hands. Whether we have open palms or we shake someone's hand, if our hearts are there, that's Methodist.

Early Methodists went to those who needed the gospel the most, not to those who wanted the gospel the most or could pay for it the best. This "neediest" Wesley maxim of mission guided Phoebe and Walter Palmer, as well as William and Catherine Booth and B. T. and Ellen Stowe Roberts in their nineteenth-century yokings of holiness, mission, and social action. The cofounder of the Salvation Army, William E. Booth, poured his life into the neediest. He lived to be an old man, but his dying words are reported to be these words of exhortation: "I want you to promise me . . . do more for the homeless of the world . . . the homeless men . . . the homeless women . . . homeless children."[36]

Can you imagine dying with that on your mind?

CHAPTER FOUR

THE SONG
OF EARTH

"The World Is My Parish":
The Method of Methodism
as a Harmonics of Hope

> *Do you have eyes but fail to see,*
> *and ears but fail to hear?*
> *And don't you remember?*
> —Jesus[1]

The essence of art is to find yourself by losing yourself at the same time. Every disciple of Jesus is an artist of life. Sometimes the greater a work of art, the longer it takes. It took five hundred years to grow one sycamore tree on the grounds of Aullwood Gardens (Ohio). It took eighteen million years to grow the Grand Canyon in Arizona. It took ten years for Michelangelo to paint the Sistine Chapel. It takes a lifetime to grow a soul.

Each artist has a "gift"—an "eye" for beauty, an "ear" for music, a "feel" for form, a "memory" for the nuances of touch and spatial detail. But the artist's gift is nothing without a commission. As French novelist Émile Zola (1840–1902) put it, "If you ask me what I came to do in this world, I, an artist, I will answer you: 'I am here to live out loud.'"[2]

Living as a "serious" follower of Jesus, in Wesley's mind, was "living out" the life of Christ in the world and "living out loud" the good life and good news—teaching the world to sing and dance, and knowing what the good life really is. For John Wesley, prevening and justifying grace did not necessarily signify a Christ-filled, Christ-breathed, Christ-lived life. Without living out Christ's life in loud acts of everyday love and mercy, one could not grow in sanctifying grace. To be a follower of Jesus meant giving 100 percent of yourself each day to "taking on the mind of Christ," which Wesley called being made "perfect in Christ." A little-j follower found one's identity in, of, and through the Meaning of Life, which is Jesus the Christ, the Big-J, the source of all meaning in life.

Christian discipleship is a pilgrimage of holiness. But every artist knows that to strive for perfection requires not just the "gift," but the honoring of that gift with a calling to mission and a call to practice makes perfect. A "writer" who doesn't write is a writer in name only. A Christian who does not "live out loud" the life of Christ is a Christian in name only. The art of following Jesus makes living holy, and makes holiness a life.

The "method" in Method-ism was all about making things holy, creating a little-j identity, living out the passion of Big-J, practicing the art of holiness. Methodism is more than a mere routine, ritual, rules of order, or general rules to follow. It is a passionate practicing of beauty, truth, and goodness in the world—a practice-makes-perfect "poetic" of holiness.

God gives no linen, but flax to spin.
—German proverb

For Wesley, attaining and maintaining holiness in life required three things: memory, practice, and passion. Like any artist, one had to re-member "within"—re-membering Christ's saving gift, sacrificial passion, and incarnational presence through what Wesley called "means of grace." In this way, you develop sensory and spiritual muscle memory.

But one also had to re-member "without"—to practice those means of grace in the world to ensure social muscle memories and to incarnate challenging lives of holiness and love. The "without" was as important as the "within," because muscle memory can work against you as well as for you. Muscle memory can't distinguish between good or bad. Without the accountability of a community, you may just be getting better at hitting wrong notes, playing mediocre music, or worse.

As every parent knows, the more passionate your kids are about their instruments, the more their practice is a joy and not a job, a pleasure and not a burden, a pull and not a push. When someone is passionate about their practice, it is almost as if that person's soul is on fire.

Methodism inculcated an aspiration for holiness that made the dream of perfection not a drive but a delight, not an enforced ritual but an enchanting experience. Wesley brought together the objective understanding of Jesus with a subjective experience of Jesus that few movements have equaled, much less excelled.

We shall never have a perfect social life, yet we must seek it
with faith. . . . The Kingdom of God is always but coming.
—Walter Rauschenbusch's closing words to
Christianity and the Social Crisis (19)[3]

But how does one keep the passion in practice and not just in performance? How does a musician take joy in recognizing unique patterns of music without getting caught up in the patterning of musicianship? A musician who simply copies a master may be technically accurate, structurally sound. But he or she will never be a true musician, nor an original artist, nor a passionate creator, but only a derivative paper doll. It takes more than technical skills and disciplined knowledge to fuel passion. It takes the imaginative living of your art.

For those following Jesus passionately in their daily lives, it takes an emotional connection, an experiential identification, a sensory awareness, a creative imagination, a spiritual engagement with the living Christ. For Wesley, the "Method" of Methodism was never meant to be an organizational scheme, but a missional, relational, and incarnational regimen of living Christ out loud in every part of life. Methodists didn't just spout Jesus, they shouted Jesus, and everyone who met them saw Jesus in them.

In the 1940s and 1950s, "method" acting revolutionized the theater and movie arts. The new way of portraying characters was taught most famously at the legendary Actors Studio in New York City by Lee Strasberg. Others soon followed. Method acting, sometimes known simply as "the Method," uses techniques such as sense and memory to create a more true or real character. The actors don't simply portray the character but become the character by taking on the character's personality and living out that role, often offscreen as well as on camera.

In other words, the actors merge their own identity with that of another. They summon their own emotions from similar events in their past in order to bring new depth to the part they are playing. No technical forms or lessons are used in teaching the "Method." But the actors practice recalling their own past experiences, and sound the depths of those emotions, applying them imaginatively to the scene they are playing in the present. Many actors have taken this so far that they would not step out of character until the movie was completed. Dustin Hoffman once went without bathing and sleeping for two days in order to immerse himself in a role.[4]

The raw emotion and sensitivity seen in "Method actors" have had more impact on the stage and screen than the more surface-style portrayals used in classical acting techniques. Whereas in classical acting, actors would use external means, such as facial expressions or voice intonations, to simulate a character, in Method acting, personal identification with the character is paramount. Free of clichés, Method acting allows actors the creative practice of drawing upon their own emotions and memories. In order to perfect this style of acting, various exercises and practices involving sense and memory are used. These help to connect the character intimately with his or her sensual experiences and to make him or her more aware of the passions that drive human actions. And the actors are taught to connect with one another on a very intimate level throughout the performance. Sanford Meisner of the Group Theatre calls this "living truthfully under imaginary circumstances"—a "poetics" of acting in which life becomes art.[5]

In Method acting, you don't impersonate a character. You personate a character. The "Method" of Methodism calls for J-followers to personate, not impersonate, Jesus; to "live out" and "live out loud" the life of Christ in the world; to become little-j's who embody the Big-J. For Wesley, holiness was not simulacrum, but incarnation; not analogy, but actualization; not act, but actual.

To follow Jesus means more than walking in the footsteps of Jesus, the illustrious teacher, or speaking with his tongue. Jesus is not a hero to be emulated and put on some pedestal, admired from afar. Methodism was not in the business of incubating a message, but incarnating the Messenger. Holiness was not working harder to mimic Jesus, but was to manifest Jesus. A life of holiness was not the imitation of Christ, but the impartation of Christ through the implantation of the Holy Spirit, who connects us to Christ's resurrection presence and power. When the Three become One in you, transcendence becomes immanence. Then you know the "kingdom come." Then you know joy, and bliss, and heaven.

To live out holiness in life as Wesley intended, to engage in the "Method" of Methodism, is to merge our own identity with that of Jesus, so that we live a Jesus life and enjoy a deeper and deeper share in his life, death, and resurrection. That's what makes us "Christian," a little-j. His risen life flows into us, and he ministers to others through us. In practicing regularly Wesley's means of grace, we immerse ourselves relationally and spiritually in the practice, passion, and memory of the way, truth, and life of Jesus. Like Strasberg's Method, Wesley's Method revolutionized the way we live out our faith in life. Methodism, the way it was intended to be—missional, relational, incarnational—lives and breathes the Holy Spirit until a Methodist's breathing and Christ's heartbeat are one, not two.

All there is to rebooting the Wesleyan witness is found in its most famous hymn. Indeed, everything we've talked about in this book is here in miniaturized form. We usually zip right through the song, zinging others with its words as we go. But this time, I want you to read it as slowly as you can, as if you've never been introduced to it before. And maybe you haven't.

The first thing to notice is whom the song is about. Almost all of Charles Wesley's hymns focus on Jesus, whom he called the "New, Best Name of Love."[6]

> O for a thousand tongues to sing
> My dear Redeemer's Praise!
> The Glories of my God and King,
> The triumphs of His grace.

My gracious Master, and my God,
  Assist me to proclaim,
To spread through all the earth abroad,
  The honours of Thy Name.

Jesus, the name that charms our fears,
  That bids our sorrows cease;
'Tis music in the sinner's ears,
  'Tis life, and health, and peace!

He breaks the power of cancel'd sin,
  He sets the prisoner free;
His blood can make the foulest clean,
  His blood avail'd for me.

He speaks, and listening to his voice,
  New life the dead receive,
The mournful, broken hearts rejoice,
  The Humble Poor *believe*.

Hear him, ye deaf; His praise, ye dumb,
  Your loosen'd tongues employ;
Ye blind, behold your Savior come;
  And leap, ye lame, for Joy.[7]

The meaning of the name Israel is not clear. Ask any Jewish child going through bar mitzvah or bat mitzvah studies, and he or she will tell you that the Hebrew name *Israel* means "struggles with God." It derives from Genesis 32 where Jacob wrestles with the angel of God, and then is named Israel.

But there is a minority report that says *Israel* also means something else. In this nonetymological rendition, "Israel" combines two Hebrew words, *shir el*, which means "the song of God." The "struggle with God" creates the "song of God."

You could even say this "song of God" is composed of four-part harmony, corresponding with God's four-letter name: YHVH.[8] When sung on four levels, the Song of Songs is a song of *shlomo*, a song of peace and wholeness.

To rediscover our song, the essence of what it means to be Wesleyan and even United Methodist in this twenty-first-century world, is to reconnect to the elements of our song. The roots of our song will be the harmonics of our hope.

In a sense, they are connectional apps, elements to live by, re-membrances, the re-membering of our tribe. Methodism can again be the vibrancy of our lives, as Jesus is the music of our spirits.

It all starts with a song. And all songs have basic elements. This is our story. This is our song.

THE HARMONICS OF HOPE

When Wesley was asked why God raised up Methodism, he gave three reasons: First, to "save souls" or make followers of Jesus. Second, to "reform the larger church" or incarnate a body of Christ that can inculcate and incubate discipleship. Third, to "spread scriptural holiness," which Wesley dubbed the "grand depositum" and defined as "holiness of heart and life."[9]

This is the Methodist version of Jesus' MRI operating system for faith: "Go into all the world" (Missional) and "make disciples" (Relational) of "all cultures" (Incarnational).[10] Every tribe expresses the MRI differently. For example, the Lay Community of Saint Benedict invites all disciples of Jesus to express "three charisms" in our daily lives. The "three charisms" are "holy communion, holy space, holy service."[11] This is the Benedictine way of speaking of Jesus' MRI. In response to the call of Christ, we seek to live in holy communion (live incarnationally), create holy space (live relationally), and offer holy service (live missionally).

Methodism's version of Jesus' MRI is a harmonics of hope: (1) "save souls" (relational); (2) "reform the church" (incarnational); and (3) "spread scriptural holiness" (missional).

The "good news" is the story of the life, death, and resurrection of Jesus. But the good news "story" is less a genre than an attitude, less a position than a posture, less a doctrine than a dance, less a statement than a song.

The nine elements of song are melody, lyrics, harmony, tempo, rhythm, voices, dynamics, key, and practice. When we sing the Lord's song in the Wesleyan Way, these elements of sound theology keep our identity not just a matter of methodical rules but a musical method of grace.

THE GIFT OF MELODY

On resurrection morning, Mary Magdalene returned to the tomb, where her tear-clouded eyes saw two angels sitting there. They said to her, "Woman, why are you weeping?" She said to them, "They have taken away my Lord, and I do not know where they have laid him."[12] How many of our churches have taken away our Lord, and we cannot find where they have laid him?

The melody of our faith is Jesus, "the true light, which enlightens everyone."[13] The *cantus firmus* of faith is Jesus the Christ, the light that shines on everyone, and the new relationship with God made possible in the death and resurrection of Christ. Call it prevenient grace, or general revelation, or moral conscience, God's love reaches out to everyone, everywhere, every day, every way.[14] To say this gets an eye roll or an earful. But say this we must.

In Wesley's hymns, we hear the passions articulate Christ's passion magnificently, and we cheer their victory over sin and death.

Methodists have always put more emphasis on the heavenly than on the hellish. The Wesley brothers did better at writing Easter hymns than Good Friday ones. Isaac Watts may have made up for what he thought to be their deficiencies, but the true Methodist melody is a celebration—a hallelujah chorus celebrating Easter morning, "the day death died."[15]

Christ's death is our death's death. Christ's resurrection life is our life's life. This is the key element of our song.

> *If you want to know who God is, look at Jesus. If you want to know what it means to be human, look at Jesus. If you want to know what love is, look at Jesus. If you want to know what grief is, look at Jesus. And go on looking until you're not just a spectator, but you're actually part of the drama which has him as the central character.*
> —*N. T. Wright*[16]

THE GIFT OF LYRICS

A melody has lyrics. Lyrics tell stories, not verses, not points, not sayings. Scripture is not a collection of sixty-six books, a "*bibliotheca sacra*" or "library of sacred literature." The Bible is not even "one book." Rather, it is "one story." The Bible is the greatest story never told.

The Bible is the coherent narrative round the theme of redemption, the story of a journey from garden to garden city, and from blessing to loss and curse and back again to grace and bounty . . . a series of linked stories about what it means to be "in covenant" with God and to live in divine presence.

To find Methodism's renewed voice is to learn our story well enough to turn the story into song, and then to sing that song so that others resonate with that song, find their place in that song, and then together write the next verse.

Saint Thomas Aquinas is reputed to have employed the phrase "*hominem unius libri timeo*" (meaning "I fear the man of a single book"). Aquinas's phrase was consciously turned on its head by John Wesley, who informed John Newton that it was "in 1730 I began to be *homo unius libri*, to study (comparatively) no book but the Bible."[17] He wrote privately on another occasion: "I receive the written word as the whole and sole rule of my faith."[18] In fact, Wesley liked the phrase so much he used it publicly in the preface to his collected sermons: "God himself has condescended to teach the way; for this very end he came from heaven and he came from heaven; He hath written it down in a book. O give me that Book! At any price, give me the Book of God. I have it; here is knowledge enough for me. Let me be *homo unius libri*!"[19]

For Methodism to recapture its song, its people need to become again *homo unius libri* (a people of one book).

But Wesley never isolated this "one book" from all other books.

For example, this "one book" for Wesley both kept Jesus in and let him out. The Scriptures definitively reveal Christ in all his truth. But not in all his glory and goodness. We need to look around for that. But we know what to look for only because of this "one book."

Methodism refuses to separate three things: Scripture, Jesus, and the Holy Spirit. The three form a braid of incredible strength and power. But if one strand becomes separated from the other, the whole braid becomes unraveled. If the Spirit is still speaking through the Scriptures, then we will hear things about Jesus we never heard before. Or saw. Or felt. Or appreciated. The Word is made flesh is made fresh— Fresh Bread.

A "one book" person doesn't read just one book. Wesley was the kind of person who was constantly saying, "Have you read this? Have you read that?" In fact, Wesley dispensed a fortune for his day in buying books for his itinerants. He even almost made "loving to read" a requirement for being a Methodist, and organized the week into daily reading categories of literature.

Wesley would read anybody, and learn from anybody. His "plunder the Egyptians" methodology meant that he was always reading at least two books: God's Book and Pharaoh's book; the Scriptures and . . . the Huffington Post, *The Wall Street Journal, The New York Times* best-seller list, and so on. Wesley was not only concerned with hearing God's song within the world, but with singing that song together for every time and place. "The world is my parish" defined the "who" and the "where" God's message needed to be lived and sung out loud. As Jesus is the melody running through all of life, our lyrics (our life out loud) call attention to the Holy Spirit's work within the world, and the presence of a living Christ with an ongoing story that is always the same and always new.

As little-j people, we are the singers of the Jesus song. The lyrics of the melody? "I Love to Tell the Story of Jesus and His Love."

THE GIFT OF HARMONY

If historian Russell Richey is right that early Methodists spoke four "languages" at the same time (popular evangelical, Wesleyan, episcopal, republican),[20] what made Methodism multilingual and not babelian was its harmonic lushness and harmonization of difference.

Harmonization is not union or agreement, but it restores flow and concord from mundane monotones and clamorous bedlam. Harmony is the real pulchrinomics, the economics of beauty, where every passionate and connective relationship is a microcosm of the Christ relationship. Heaven-sent harmonies are those that take the most unlikely and conflicted of relationships and wind them together in exquisite harmony—all in tune with the sacramental body of Christ.

Expert tap dancers know that their best rhythms come from listening and re-creating the everyday sounds of living. What makes the dance an art is the ability to combine all of those mundane sounds in ways that sound unique and beautiful. Sound theology is not only a true, good, and beautiful theology but a theology of doxology—listening to one another and creating a quality of sound that magnifies Christ's voice, resonating God's praises in a multitude of divergent and variegated voices.

If there is one thing historians agree on regarding the first Christians, it is this: Jesus' first followers were "strikingly diverse, and disagreed about nearly everything."[21] Yet it was from this turbulent and troublesome diversity that the first Christians shaped their theological order. John Wesley knew that every person would experience Jesus' love differently. In this way, every person would bring unique gifts and perspectives to the body of Christ. Sound theology is the ability of many unique and colorful strands to be woven into a beautiful harmonic weave: it is the beauty of complexity and ecstasy that moves us beyond words. Harmony is the creative force of the universe, the intelligence of the Creator Three-in-One.

Johann Sebastian Bach was famous for his two-part, three-part, and more-part musical inventions. The genius of the "invention" was to bring together several progressions of sound and variation, each with distinctive turns, rhythms, and grace notes and to combine them into a stunning harmonic masterpiece.

In a sense, the body of Christ is God's ultimate musical masterpiece. It demonstrates above all the divine harmony and wholeness of relationships within the human realm. It is the bride of Christ and the foretaste of God's kingdom, the harmony of the heavens and a revelation of the mystery of God and God's MRI self.

We can be bound together but move separately and differently. Harmony can sometimes move with occasional notes of dissonance, with clashes of sound, with at times a random voice slightly out of tune, with any number of voices joining the music, as long as it moves together, and at the direction of the Divine Composer.

One of my favorite anthems is "Thou Shalt Know Him When He Comes" based on these lines by Forceyth Willson:

> Thou shalt know him, when he comes, . . .
> Not by any din of drums,
> Nor the vantage of his airs,
> Neither by his crown,
> Nor his gown,
> Nor by anything he wears.
> He shall only well-known be,
> By the holy harmony
> That his coming makes in thee![22]

The best spiritual practice I can think of is to sing in a choir—whether a community choir, church choir, or some other kind of choir—because it schools the soul in harmonious difference. In a choir, we learn *not* to sing the same notes, *not* to sing the same words, *not* to sing the same beat, even at times *not* to sing on the same page, but to sing the same song.

Warren Bennis famously defined leadership as "the capacity to create a compelling vision and translate it into action and sustain it."[23] Following Jesus is about the ability to find one's voice and to hear and call other voices into harmonious mission. It is not to rival whose voice can be heard the loudest or to attempt to vie for the Conductor's job.

Wesley's Methodism is a harmonic masterpiece of connective passion. It is one true voice of the body of Christ in the world today.

One might even say the social neurons are packed more densely in the Methodist brain than others. Density fosters faster links and connectedness, yielding trigger-happy synapses. A dead church has a social brain that isn't throbbing. An alive church isn't without headaches, but its brain is pounding from "chains of inspiration,"[24] which spark one another and boost creativity and social synergy, leading to phase, and life, transitions. All of which lead to the gift of "holy harmony."

THE GIFT OF DYNAMICS

In the news industry, bad news is good news, and good news is no news.

Methodists are people who megaphone the "good news." Dynamics in music are the degrees of volume and intensity invested by the musician, and experienced by the receiver. Dynamics are those things that draw attention to our song and give it a life and style beyond the monotony of mere mechanics. Dynamics give attitude to the music. Each life-song has a dynamic of its own. And that life-song tells a story. Each story is a tribute to the presence and power of Jesus.

A dynamic faith is the opposite of a "mechanical" faith, one more invested in rules and routines than in passion and suspense. Instead of a marionette show of high order, a dynamic faith is an organic fluctuation and flow from the original fountainhead of the tradition: it moves in spurts and sputters; it emits sparks and syncopation; it raises its voice at times; it refuses just "going through the motions." Dynamic faith can be seen and heard. Dynamic faith exudes spirit, whether spiccato, pizzicato, or vibrato. When we live faith in the Wesleyan Way, the dynamics of volume and intensity enable our song to be heard over the tumult to touch our culture. To embrace the gift of dynamics is to ask ourselves whether we know our song well enough and love our song deeply enough to sing it "out loud" and crescendo to *f* (forte), *ff* (fortissimo), or even sometimes *fff* (fortissississimo).

A dynamic faith is never static. Dynamics change within a piece of music. Dynamics enhance the expressive qualities of a song and require some kind of response from the listener. Varying the dynamics draws attention to revelatory moments and to rubato expressions that increase awareness of the message of the music.

The deliberate use of silent intervals is an important component of dynamics. Living out loud requires times of pause and intermission; pauses not only to stay tuned with the Creator/Composer of Life, but determined pauses that make the experience of living out loud plausible. All strains of music breathe. Dynamic faith both inhales and exhales the breath of the Holy Spirit. In order to sing life's loudest and most "lusty" phrases, one must pause to take breaths.

Jesus began his ministry turning water into wine at the marriage feast. For the early Methodists, this meant more than Jesus wanting to turn the water of dull religion into the sparkling wine of experiential faith. It meant that the numbing of the familiar was smashed forever by the everyday surprises of the Spirit. The True Vine makes wine out of water every day in grapes. Followers of Christ, when we are grafted into the Vine, bear fruit in the hope that God will make wine out of us all. This is one of the most beautiful metaphors for discipleship Jesus ever offered: bearing fruit every year until it becomes positively ordinary, a miracle of the everyday. Or in Charles Wesley's own words:

> When wine they want, the Almighty Lord
> Water instead of wine demands.
> He both created by His Word,
> Nothing His sovereign power withstands,
> And every year in every vine
> He changes water into wine.[25]

Dynamic discipleship flows with the water of the Spirit and tastes like the wine of Christ. The dynamic of living a little-j life means that we are not only bearing fruit, but fruit fresh from the vine. It is not enough that Jesus gets our heart juices flowing. Only in heart fermentation can the Spirit produce within us what it takes to be wine and blood.

The dynamics of discipleship require starting power and staying power—not only a fresh-rooted faith but a faith willing to invest time and space in depth and maturity. Only in this sanctifying process of fermentation will our water be "perfected" into wine. The longer and more deeply we immerse ourselves in the mind of Christ, the more our dynamics will reflect the mindfulness of the Master.

> *Sky is the daily bread of the eyes.*
> *—Ralph Waldo Emerson*[26]

Every good thing can be overdone. Methodism drew a line between experience and emotionality, or what was then called "enthusiasm." When faith becomes too subjective, too inward focused, and goes off on its own way without reining in by Scripture and tradition, our music becomes without form and void, "full of sound and fury, signifying nothing."[27] Our dynamics must always emerge from, and not float free from, the disciplines of melody. Dynamics without melody or lyrics or harmony is barren.

To live a dynamic faith with intensity and passion opens one to criticism. "Love your enemies" doesn't mean "Don't make any." The more dynamic your faith, the more you will draw the attention of those who are threatened by your passion, people who will do and say anything to hush your song. Whoever lives their story out loud in the world, and sings their song over the din of mediocrity, makes an inviting target for critics, hatchet-job haters, and razor-bladed religion.

> *It's good to know who hates you, and it's*
> *good to be hated by the right people.*
> —*Johnny Cash*[28]

The Wesley of tricorn hat, high horse, and peruke (powered wig) drew the fire and ire of many enemies. It didn't help that Wesley's love life was a lifelong disaster. Early on, Moravian James Hutton wrote in 1740 that the Wesley brothers, "both of them, are dangerous snares to many young women; several are in love with them."[29] Things hadn't changed much over the course of a lifetime. Preacher John Pawson wrote these words in 1791: "His greatest Weakness was his extreme fondness of the company of agreeable young women. Not that there was anything criminal in this. But in him it was an inexcusable weakness. He let himself down in the esteem of those who knew him the best exceedingly, and often he grieved them beyond measure."[30]

Wesley was at the same time viciously attacked for being papist, and attacked by the papists. There were those who saw in Wesley's Methodism covert popery and the Roman Catholic confessional closeted in the class meeting. But for those critics who accused Methodism of being crypto-Catholic, it didn't make any difference when Catholic bishop Richard Challoner went on a vehement attack against the Methodists (1760), in which Wesley and his preachers were castigated as "ministers of Satan," "false prophets," "wolves in sheep's clothing," and their societies "synagogues of Satan."[31]

How many Christians do you know with souls soaked in venom, their spirits spewing out plagues of hatred and self-righteousness, with their hanging faces interested only in silencing others, not exploring truth together; in hating others, not loving others? When our passion becomes more for our religion, our own worldview, our institutional survival than for Christ, the more we gouge, scratch, scrape, and jab.

If you sing with a high-volume voice, you will be mocked and maligned. Methodism is a high-volume faith. Methodists speak out and live out loud. So be warned: to restore the dynamic of a Wesleyan faith is to contend with the dynamics of hatred and attacks.

THE GIFT OF RHYTHM

The presence of a particular rhythm may help to identify a specific musical genre. Rhythm shows uniqueness, singularity, and distinctive patterns in our walk and talk with Jesus.

In music, rhythm may be defined as the pattern or placement of sounds in time and beats in music: more formally, rhythm is "the particular arrangement of note lengths in a piece of music."[32] Rhythm is framed by meter, but it is grounded in beat and tempo. Rhythm is the creativity that arises from discipline. Whereas our walk with Jesus is guardrailed by texts and traditions, our personal expression and experience of that walk bear a unique gait, a rhythm and pace distinct to each of us.

The rhythm of our faith will reflect the ways in which we embody the discipline in our discipleship. For some, it may mean times of meditation interspersed with times of study, prayer, praise, and fasting (Wesley fasted at least one day a week all his life). Others may seek new and creative rhythms of discipleship, such as social media, running, painting, or gardening. Each rhythm dedicated to God is a beautiful variation and creative syncopation within the meter of our faith and the heartbeat of our little-j "body" of Christ.

Methodism itself has a distinctive rhythm—a way of walking with Jesus, of living in step with the living Christ. Wesley was all about getting the rhythm right, and he spent his life generating resources to help people get in sync with the Spirit.

Rhythm is the gait of our journey. Where the Anglican Church was running in place, Wesley took Christians on a journey, and he took the church places it had never meant to go. Maybe our desire to "take a stand" on the issues of the day needs to be replaced with a mentality of "taking a hike" on the path of God's mission in the world.

The beauty of rhythm is that it does not negate meter, but creatively stretches beyond it in order to make distinctive the song of Jesus.

Charles Simeon (1759–1836) was a brilliant young leader of the Calvinist revival. At twenty-five years of age, Simeon arranged an interview with the octogenarian John Wesley to talk about Wesley's Arminianism and his belief that Jesus died for all (and not just for the elect). The "interview" took place on December 20, 1784:

> A young minister, about three or four years after he was ordained, had an opportunity of conversing familiarly with the great and venerable leader of the Arminians in this kingdom, and, wishing to improve the occasion, he addressed him nearly in the following words: "Sir, I understand that you are called an Arminian; and I have been sometimes called a Calvinist; and therefore I suppose we are to draw daggers. But before I consent to begin the combat, with your permission I will ask you a few questions." Permission being very readily and kindly granted, the young minister proceeded to ask: "Pray, Sir, do you feel yourself a depraved creature, so depraved that you would never have thought of turning to God, if God had not first put it into your heart?" "Yes," says the veteran, "I do indeed." "And do you utterly despair of recommending yourself to God by anything you can do; and look for salvation solely through the blood and righteousness of Christ?" "Yes, solely through Christ." "But, Sir, supposing you were at first saved by Christ, are you not somehow or other to save yourself afterwards by your own works?" "No, I must be saved by Christ from first to last." "Allowing, then, that you were first turned by the grace of God, are you not in some way or other to keep yourself by your own power?" "No."
>
> "What then, are you to be upheld every hour and every moment by God, as much as an infant in its mother's arms?" "Yes, altogether." "And is all your hope in the grace and mercy of God to preserve you unto His heavenly kingdom?" "Yes, I have no hope but in Him." "Then, Sir, with your leave I will

put up my dagger again; for this is all my Calvinism; this is my election, my justification by faith, my final perseverance: it is in substance all that I hold, and as I hold it; and therefore, if you please, instead of searching out terms and phrases to be a ground of contention between us, we will cordially unite in those things wherein we agree."[33]

Wesley tipped his hat to the young man's spirit and fervor in his *Journal*.[34] Or in the words found in Wesley's sermon "A Catholic Spirit" (1771), "If your heart is as my heart, if you love God and all mankind, I ask no more: 'give me your hand.' "[35]

Of all the words Wesley spoke or wrote, those perhaps have most struck a chord from generation to generation.

THE GIFT OF TEMPO

Methodists were not "free spirits," but freed spirits. That freedom of a "freed spirit" is what gave the Wesleyan tribe an upbeat tempo.

Methodists have always sung their hearts out. For Wesley, the "ideal Christian life was one of ceaseless, cheerful activism."[36] But this upbeat tempo is not the result of some head-in-the-clouds optimism, but some groundwater hope. Edward St. Aubyn's novel that concludes the Melrose series *At Last* (2011) has this satirical line that really hurts: thinking about Jesus, the character Patrick supposes that "it must be hard to be chosen as optimism's master cliché, the Light at the End of the Tunnel, ruling over a glittering army of half-full glasses and silver-lined clouds."[37] Methodists are not so much "optimistic" as hopeful, a hope grounded in the promises of God even while gazing into the hidden recesses of the human heart. The Wesleyan Way of hope brings realism to reality.

Happiness lay in a relationship with Christ based not on a Christ whom we grasp only in our minds, but a Christ who speaks to us in our hearts and minds through his living presence and activity. The jaunty meter of John Wesley's journey stemmed from his assurance that the heartbeat of Jesus gives abundant life here and eternal life to come.

The Methodist body has a racing pulse. The pulse of the Wesleyan heart is high energy, reflecting a relentless activism ever on the way and moment-notice ready for mission. The driving tempo of Methodism is excited by Christ and excited about life. It thrives on change and challenges.

A tribe in Central Asia uses a strange curse against their neighbors. They don't say, "Go to hell!" They say, "May you stay in one place forever," which may be another way of saying the same thing. Boredom and blandness are the terrible curse of the unvarying.

Tempo guides how fast the piece of music will be played and is usually constant throughout a selection, although deliberate tempo changes may be used for dramatic effect. Methodism has a distinct beat, a unique tempo, in sync with the winds of the Spirit. Methodists in Wesley's day were quick *to* their feet and fast *on* their feet. They were masters of both the *carpe diem* and the *carpe mañana*. This does not mean that Methodism has not played its song in every tempo, including slow (adagio), fast (allegro), moderate (moderato), and very fast (presto). Methodism famously adapts to any culture, lives in any host. But its unique charisma lies in its agility in ventriloquizing the voice of Jesus and changing hearts with his song.

John Wesley had such personal charisma and could so mesmerize a crowd that even when a large cat, spooked by some noise, leaped out a window, landed on a woman's head, and bounced from head to head, bounding up and down shoulders and backs, the crowd remained calm, and no one cried out.[38]

Today we suffer from the opposite of charisma, a condition that might be called "amsirahc"—"charisma" spelled backwards. Our "amsirahc" is built on a suasive and suave set of principles. Our lost "charisma" was built on the spirit of Christ. Our "amsirahc" is built on "Trust the Process." Our "charisma" was built on "Trust the Spirit." Think about this: Paul traveled one thousand kilometers with Silas without knowing where they were going. They had no plan, no blueprint, just a trust in God and the Spirit to take them where they needed to go.

Singing in sync with the Spirit means joining in Christ's MRI song, embarking on Christ's missional journey, no matter where it takes us. We improvise and innovate as we go, following the fire by night and the cloud (windblown water) by day. We supply the voices, but God creates the symphony. We sing at the direction of our Conductor. We follow his meter, his beat, his tempo—and in faith, we let go and become his music.

The heartbeat of Methodism is mission. The Wesleyan song is metered in ¾ time: three in one person, and fourscore in mission.

THE GIFT OF KEY

Methodism is no miniaturized faith. Methodists do not move by drift, but by big dreams and grand designs. And the biggest dream of Methodism is "perfect love." Methodists are people who sing in the key of love.

Jesus didn't say to love someone because that person is lovely. Jesus said it is love that makes a person lovely. So love. "Everyone will know that you are my disciples, if you have love for one another."[39] Technically, there are no "I Do's" in the wedding service. The words are "I Will." The covenant of love is an act of will.

Touched by the lodestone of thy love,
let all our hearts agree,
and ever toward each other move,
and ever move toward thee.
—"Jesus, United by Thy Grace"[40]

God's love is "perfected" in and among us, the Bible says.[41] In other words, God's love is a verb that fulfills its mission in and among the body. And that mission in part is to help us achieve "the measure of the full stature of Christ."[42]

It isn't enough for followers of Jesus to discipline their voices by learning musical theory or by practicing in their own modalities. To be pitch-perfect is to sing in the right key. Jesus sets the key. And the key for Jesus is always love.

Faith, hope, and love are the ringtones of discipleship. These three ringtones that signify the cultivated religious mind cannot exist apart from one another, with the sole exception of Christ, who has no need for faith or hope because he is "perfect Love" (*perfecta caritas*).[43] "And the greatest of these is love."[44] How do we key up our voices to perfect love? How do we find and sustain that key?

Gratitude.

In Wesley's younger days at Lincoln College in Oxford, there was a porter who knocked on his door one evening and asked to speak with him. After some conversation Wesley noted the man's thin coat on such a cold night. Wesley suggested that he had better get another coat. The porter replied, "This coat . . . is the only coat I have in the world, and I thank God for it."

Wesley then asked the man if he had eaten and the porter replied, "I have had nothing today but a draught of springwater . . . and I thank God for that."

Wesley now was growing uneasy in the man's presence. He reminded the porter that he would need to hurry on and get to his quarters or risk being locked out. "Then what would you have to thank God for?" Wesley asked.

"I'll thank him," the porter replied, "that I have dry stones to lie upon."

Wesley became deeply moved by this man's piety, and said to him, "You thank God when you have nothing to wear, and you thank him when you have nothing to eat, and you thank him when you have no bed to lie on. I cannot see what you have to thank him for."

The man replied, "I thank him . . . that he has given me life and being; and a heart to love him, and a desire to serve him."

Wesley sent the man away with a coat from his closet, some money for food, and words of gratitude for his witness. But, as John Reynolds recorded, that experience convinced Wesley "that there was something in religion with which he was unacquainted and it made a lasting impression on his mind."[45]

Gratitude is love in the key of faith and hope.

"Ya gotta have faith" is no mere pious banter or devout bromide. Without faith, it is impossible to please God.[46] Faith does not always bring victory but faith IS the victory: "This is the victory that has overcome the world, even our faith."[47]

Our morality is not only our choices but our vision.
—*Iris Murdoch*[48]

God must do something *in* us before God can do something mighty *through* us. In order for us to impart God's love to the world through our song, we must first sing in key. When we allow God to set the key, our song becomes more enchanting.

Love is a verb that expresses not rules but relationships. In our focus on social justice, we must be careful that we don't focus on doing more than being, on Christian activism more than Christian faith. In the entire Lord's Prayer, there is only one activity that we do: "as we forgive those who trespass against us."

As fragrance is to flower, so good works is to faith. For Methodism, faith is hope with a long neck and love with a strong back. But works do not enfaith, faith frames works. In fact, works are the death mask of a living faith. Jesus left the poor not with money, but with rich hope. Jesus left the oppressed not with the right to vote, but with rich faith. Jesus left the lonely not with lovers, but with rich love. In terms of the church, Faith defines it, Love binds it, Hope drives it. Hope is a kind of heart stimulant, the digitalis of love.

There are forces in this universe, fields of energy. Love is one of them. Creative intelligence is another. We can send one another energy. Atoms do it all the time. When we navigate the energies of love and creative intelligence, whenever we have linked intellectual firepower to spiritual horsepower, there has been in history a force field of holiness that changed the world.

It's time to do it again.

THE GIFT OF PRACTICE

As we have seen, the "Method" in "Methodist" is most seen as "methodical," organized, systematized. But Wesley meant something more than this. He meant a growth in holiness, an intensification of "perfect love," a deepening of one's identity in Christ so that each person becomes a little-j. The mark of good "method" is not efficiency, but quality—the character and caliber of beauty, meaning, and complexity.

In the document Wesley called "The Nature, Design, and General Rules of the United Societies," most commonly known as the General Rules, Wesley itemized three things expected of everyone who joined the Methodist movement:

1. Do No Harm
2. Do All the Good You Can
3. "Attend upon all the ordinances of God."[49]

That third "attend" requirement referenced the means of grace, practices that facilitate growth in Christ.

Methodists are people who "practice" their faith, people who grow closer to Jesus through daily "practice." Just because you're pursuing holy matters in your thought and research doesn't make you holy. That's what might be called "the theologian's fallacy." These "practices" or "means of grace" were of two kinds: (1) works of piety and (2) works of mercy. Works of piety are vertically focused on God: "love the Lord your God with all"[50] you have through prayer, Bible study, fasting, Holy Communion, holy conferencing, and so forth. Works of mercy are horizontally focused on others —"to be as eyes to the blind and feet to the lame; a husband to the widow, a father to the fatherless."[51] Bring works of piety and works of mercy together, and Wesley called this "practicing" the presence of God.

Each time you lift up your voice to sing, you risk failure. But when you choose to stifle your voice, you have already failed. Discipleship is a combination of "discipline" and "ship" ("ship" was Wesley's favorite metaphor for the church). To sail your ship of faith on the open seas is to risk the waves and billows. The discipline of risk does not inhibit or push down the severity of risk. But the discipline of discipleship "opens one up" to the winds of the Spirit, frees one up to take risks for Christ.

Methodism is a practice of entering into the risky seas, of hearing the beckoning sound of the winds across the waters. Jesus spoke from a boat on the waves of the sea. His voice carried over the waters asking disciples to leave the safety of the shores and follow him. Being a disciple of Jesus is not about safe harbors, but about risky faith. To practice our faith is to engage in a no-holds-barred, daily relationship with the living Lord. No song can be perfected without practice.

The Methodist symphony spirals onward. It renews and revives itself through the variant vibrations of cultures and climes. If we want to join the revival, we have to start singing our song again.

The question isn't whether or not the doomsayers of Methodism are wrong or right.

The question is, will you join the chorus?

THE GIFT OF VOICES

The one thing the early church never got right was the relation of clergy and lay. Let's start with Jesus: what was he? Whatever your answer, this is sure: at his death, he was stripped of all stature.

Clericalism is one of the worst problems any tribe can have. Clericalism leads to a lumpen laity and a clot in the pulpit that blocks the flow of the Spirit and bottlenecks creativity.

The Methodist movement propelled forward the liberation of the laity, and took the doctrine of the "priesthood of all believers" in directions where it had not gone before. We need to continue that liberation movement, and let people see their fingerprints all over whatever we are doing.

When I was starting out in ministry, I engaged in a personal crusade to bring back the "camp meeting" experience, and enlisted Willie Nelson to help me. At one event, I invited one of the top laypeople from the national church to lead a workshop on "The Laity Lead." After agreeing to do the workshop, I got this panicky letter:

> Len, in order to do appropriate planning for my workshops, as well as to be able to respond to people I am sure now will ask me what my workshops are, I need to know exactly what is expected of me. I felt somewhat "out on

a limb" having agreed to lead workshops but not knowing what you have in mind. Please write or call, so that I can feel more comfortable about my role in what promises to be an outstanding experience for our church.

Here's one of the highest-ranking laypeople in a position of leadership in The United Methodist Church, at a loss to know what to do with the theme "The Laity Lead."

In many ways, this book is an ode to eccentricity, to originality, to imagination within the institution, and to the liberation of the laity where every baptized disciple sees himself or herself as both a minister and a missionary, with a ministry to the body and a mission in the world.

The grandeur of Methodism is its multitude of voices. If we want to re-member our churches in the Wesleyan Way, we need to re-mind ourselves that we are all given the gifts of ministry and mission by our Voice-giving, Vision-casting God. But we have liked too much the sound of our own voices and too little the sounding of the voice of Truth—a voice sometimes soft, sometimes stentorian, but always steadfast.

All are powerful voices singing the harmonics of hope in "the greatest story ever told."

Give me one hundred preachers who fear nothing but sin, and desire nothing but God, and I care not a straw whether they be clergymen or laymen; such alone will shake the gates of hell and set up the kingdom of heaven on Earth.

—John Wesley[52]

INTERACTIVES

1. There are four Kinds of Christians: pooh-poohs (negative, disdainful), oom-pah-pahs (monotonous, legalistic), umphs (vital, vivacious, enthusiastic), and the blah-blah-blahs (disconnected, disoriented, indifferent). This reminds me of the old Flip Wilson quip: "I'm a Jehovah's Bystander. They invited me to be a Witness, but I didn't want to get involved." Discuss how these four kinds of Christians can either contribute to or stifle the Lord's song.

2. Jazz first appeared as ragtime, but became "jazz" during the First World War. Listen to "Rhythm Saved the World" performed by Louis Armstrong and written in 1936. Discuss how important music was to history. Some say Elvis, the Beatles, and rock music did more to bring down the Soviet Union than the U.S. military or the Soviet economy. Condemned by every Soviet regime as degenerate and a Western sickness, the "last Soviet generation" fell in love with British and American rock music. In the midst of the condemnation, this generation caught the craze of the West and began to question all the "authoritative" declarations of communist officialdom.

3. Discuss this ode to silence from Mother Teresa of Calcutta:

> We need to find God and God cannot be found in noise and restlessness. God is the friend of silence. See how nature, the trees, the flowers, the grass—grow in silence; see the stars, the moon and the sun, how they move in silence. Is not our mission to give God to the poor in the slums? Not a dead God, but a living, loving God. The more we receive in silent prayer, the more we can give in our active life. Silence gives us a new outlook on everything. We need silence to be able to touch souls. The essential thing is not what we say, but what God says to us and through us. . . . All our words will be useless unless they come from within—words which do not give the light of Christ increase the darkness.[1]

4. At the opening of *The Tempest*, Shakespeare has the seamen cry out when shipwreck seems imminent: "All is lost! To prayers! To prayers! To prayers" (act 1, scene 1). Why is it that we utter the cry "To prayers!" only when all is lost or feels that way?

5. Henrik Ibsen's drama *Brand* has the main character (Brand) struggling to make it through a desolate part of Norway in the midst of a huge blizzard. Another man sees him and cries out, "Go back, go back!" Brand replies, "I can't. I can't. I am on a mission for someone great whose name is God."[2]

Are we not all on a mission for someone great whose name is God? Describe your experience as a "missionary" of God.

6. Conrad Gempf distinguishes between a mystery and a secret in this way. A mystery book or movie mystery carries an expectation that at some point and in some way one can solve the mystery, but until then, there are "clues" that one is expected to seek out, pick up, and live with. This is in contrast to a "secret" where there is no expectation of ever getting anything.[3] How does this distinction help you understand your relationship with Christ?

7. Discuss this quote from Arnold S. Oh:

> But Jesus' call on his disciples is not a call to good citizenship. When Jesus called the first disciples working at their nets at the Sea of Galilee, he called them to leave everything and follow him. Their identity had been wrapped up in quite a lot before: occupation, family, and yes, even culture. He was calling them to a new identity. And he was calling them as the Living God who offered them no programs, no promises, and no guarantees apart from a simple invitation to come, take up the cross, and follow the Savior on his journey. "Follow me," Jesus says. "And immediately they left their nets and followed him" (Mark 1:17-18).[4]

8. Charles Wesley's most mystical hymn, "Thou Shepherd of Israel," is no longer sung. Why do you think this is so? Do you agree with those who say this is his "most fervid hymn"?

1 Thou Shepherd of Israel, and mine,
The joy and desire of my heart,
For closer communion I pine,
I long to reside where thou art:
The pasture I languish to find
Where all, who their Shepherd obey,
Are fed, on thy bosom reclined,
And screened from the heat of the day.

2 Ah! show me that happiest place,
The place of thy people's abode,
Where saints in an ecstasy gaze,
And hang on a crucified God;
Thy love for a sinner declare,
Thy passion and death on the tree:
My spirit to Calvary bear,
To suffer and triumph with thee.

3 'Tis there, with the lambs of thy flock,
There only, I covet to rest,
To lie at the foot of the rock,
Or rise to be hid in thy breast;
'Tis there I would always abide,
And never a moment depart,
Concealed in the cleft of thy side,
Eternally held in thy heart.[5]

9. The military use sound as a form of torture. Discuss the following:

The Branch Davidians in Texas were bombarded with "the recorded shrieks of dying rabbits during the 1993 siege"—strangely, as Keizer points out, "for the purpose of liberating allegedly abused children." In 1989, the Panamanian dictator Manuel Noriega was chased from his sanctuary in the Vatican Embassy with loudspeakers playing heavy metal music and hard rock songs such as "We're Not Gonna Take It" by Twisted Sister twenty-four hours a day. Also using heavy metal music (you can see a sort of military logic), the 361st PsyOps company of the U.S. Army "prepared the battle-field" during the siege of Fallujah in 2004. And Binyam Mohamed recalls that his interrogators hung him up in a "pitch black room" where there was "loud music, 'Slim Shady' and Dr. Dre, for 20 days." Other songs reportedly used to break prisoners down include Metallica's "Enter Sandman" and, less heavy and metal but perhaps even more terrible, Barney the Dinosaur's "I Love You." Keizer adds, "When a country appropriates its most popular art forms in the service of torturing its enemies, is it not admitting repulsion at its own culture? . . .Were I a suspected Muslim terrorist undergoing torture, I would hang on to that thought to steel my resolve."[6]

10. Do you know anyone who isn't an audiophile? Do you know anyone who hates music and refuses to let it into her or his life? Why do you think to be human is to be musical?

11. Discuss the changing landscape of religion in the U.S. For me that changing landscape is reflected in this one statistic: when the seminary where I teach (Drew Theological Seminary) was founded in 1867, 40 percent of the people in the U.S. were Methodist. In 2010, United Methodists are at best 8 to 9 percent, and all of "mainline"/oldline Protestantism constitutes 19 percent. The growing edge of religion in the US? Atheists, agnostics, and "don't know," who now number almost as many as old-line Protestants (17 percent).

12. There is an old saying: "Work like a Wesleyan, pray like a Calvinist." Can you unpack what that might mean? Might this Calvinist riff on a Wesleyan ditty help to explore the difference?

> Wesleyan: "Rise Up, O men of God, / Have done with lesser things. / Give heart and soul and mind and strength, / To serve the King of kings."

> Calvinist: "Sit down, O men of God, / His kingdom he will bring, / Whenever it may please his will, / You cannot do a thing."

13. If confirmation classes were to become more con-formation and in-formation courses, do you think people of the Wesleyan Way should require that this "Wesley Covenant" be memorized by every person who hails Wesley as the founder of his or her tribe?

> I am no longer my own, but thine.
> Put me to what thou wilt, rank me with whom thou wilt.
> Put me to doing, put me to suffering.

Let me be employed by thee or laid aside for thee,
exalted for thee or brought low for thee.
Let me be full, let me be empty.
Let me have all things, let me have nothing.
I freely and heartily yield all things
to thy pleasure and disposal.
And now, O glorious and blessed God,
Father, Son, and Holy Spirit,
thou art mine, and I am thine. So be it.
And the covenant which I have made on earth,
let it be ratified in heaven. Amen.

14. Check out this resource for whole-church change in the Wesleyan Way called "SoulShift." It was started by Steve Deneff and David Drury (and College Wesleyan Church): www.oursoulshift.com. Share your impressions and thoughts.

15. Have someone record "The Five," which is on every day on the Fox News Channel. Watch how the show's five personalities—always one Democrat, one Republican, and one Libertarian—will argue, affront, and sometimes almost abuse one another. What brings them back to the common table?

Watch how after every issue they debate, a musical segue of "golden oldies" transitions to the commercials and to a downtime of shared memories and sedentary dance motions. How might music enable us to fight more fairly and honestly, and still come away as friends?

16. Four angels watched God create the world:

1. "Why did God make it?" asked the first angel. This is the Catholic question.

2. "How did God make it?" asked the second angel. This is the Calvinist question.

3. "How can I get it?" asked the third angel. This is the Pentecostal question.

4. "How can I take care of it?" asked the fourth angel. This is the Wesleyan question.

To what extent is care for creation a part of your church's ministry and mission? How can you develop and deepen this ministry in your church?

NOTES

Introduction

1. John Wesley, *How to Pray: The Best of John Wesley* (Ulrichsville, Ohio: Barbour, 2007), 70.

2. For more on the "future is female," see Steve Jones, *Y: The Descent of Men* (Boston: Houghton Mifflin, 2003), esp. 28.

3. Some argue that the modern family has less "declined" than "diversified," with second families, step-families, adoptive families, same-gender families, single-parent families, and so forth.

4. George Herbert, *A Priest to the Temple, or The Countrey Parson, His Character, and Rule of Holy Life* in *The Temple and A Priest to the Temple* (London: J. M. Dent, 1908), 222.

5. The best elaboration of this concept is Philip Bobbitt, *The Shield of Achilles: War, Peace and the Course of History* (New York: Knopf, 2002); and also his *Terror and Consent: The Wars of the Twenty-First Century* (New York: Knopf, 2008).

6. See Arnold S. Oh, "Missions: Letting the Gospel Translate Us," in *Generation Rising: A Future with Hope for The United Methodist Church*, ed. Andrew C. Thompson (Nashville: Abingdon, 2011), 65. Oh's article is an excellent look at what he calls "overtranslation."

7. Augustine, "Sermon XV," in *A Select Library of the Nicene and Post-Nicene Fathers of the Church*, ed. Philip Schaff (New York: Christian Literature, 1888), 6:306.

8. Nathan Benchley, *Robert Benchley: A Biography* (New York: McGraw-Hill, 1955), 3.

9. John Gambold was a friend of the Wesleys who started out a Cambridge Methodist but became a Unitas Fratrum minister. The poetry of John Gambold must have impressed the Wesleys, as they preserved and kept in circulation his poems. John Gambold, "Upon Listening to the Vibrations of a Clock," quoted in *The Poetical Works of John and Charles Wesley: Reprinted from the Original, with the Last Corrections of the Author: Together with the Poems of Charles Wesley Not Before Published*, collected and arranged by G. Osborn (London: Wesleyan Methodist Conference Office, 1868), 1:10. Here is the rest of the poem:

How the past moment dies, and throbs no more!
What worlds of parts compose the rolling hour!
At least of these a serious care demands
For though they're little, yet they're golden sands.
By some great deeds distinguish'd all in heaven,
For the same end to me by number given!
Cease, man, to lavish sums thou ne'er hast told!
Angels, though deathless, dare not be so bold.

10. Stephen John Tonsor, *Reflections on the French Revolution: A Hillsdale Symposium* (Washington, D.C.: Regency Gateway, 1990), 20.

11. Two friends have argued that the case is even worse, that we have instituted incentives for decline, and reward the implementation of those incentives. See John Flowers and Karen Vannoy, *10 Temptations of Church: Why Churches Decline and What to Do about It* (Nashville: Abingdon, 2012).

12. Edmund Burke, *Reflections on the Revolution in France, and on the Proceedings in Certain Societies in London Relative to That Event, in a Letter Intended to Have Been Sent to a Gentleman in Paris*, 2nd ed. (London: J. Dodsley, 1790), 47–48.

13. Notice he did not say "individuals called Methodists." For more on Jesus followers as a "people" (1 Peter 2:10), see Andrew C. Thompson, "'Once You Were No People, But Now You Are God's People,'" in *Generation Rising*, 143–46.

14. Johann Wolfgang von Goethe, *William Meister's Apprenticeship*, in *Goethe's Wilhelm Meister's Apprenticeship and Travels*, trans. Thomas Carlyle, ed. Clement King Shorter (Chicago: A. C. McClurg, 1890), 2:149.

15. Kenneth Clark, *What Is a Masterpiece* (London: Thames and Hudson, 1979), 10–11.

16. Arthur Koestler, preface to *The Yogi and the Commissar and Other Essays* (New York: Macmillan, 1945), v–vi.

17. Job 3:25.

18. Mark 4:40b.

19. Martin Luther, *The Bondage of the Will*, trans. Philip S. Watson, vol. 33 of *Luther's Works* (Philadelphia: Fortress, 1972), 24.

20. 2 Corinthians 1:18–19 NIV.

21. John Wesley, "Thoughts on Methodism," in *The Methodist Societies: History, Nature, and Design*, ed. Rupert E. Davies, vol. 9 of *The Works of John Wesley* (Nashville: Abingdon, 1989), 527.

1. The Song of Water

1. Isaac Watts, "Our Frail Bodies, and God Our Preserver," in *Hymns and Spiritual Songs, Book II: Composed on Divine Subjects*, in *The Works of the Late Reverend and Learned Isaac Watts* (London: Printed for T. and T. Longman, 1753), 4:205.

2. John Wesley, "A Treatise on Baptism," in *The Miscellaneous Works of the Rev. John Wesley* (New York: J. & J. Harper, 1828), 2:155, 157–58.

3. The ban was not lifted until 1967.

4. D. H. Lawrence, "Hymns in a Man's Life," in *Late Essays and Articles*, ed. James T. Boulton (Cambridge: Cambridge University Press, 2004), 132.

5. Ibid., 130.

6. Medieval artists painted Mary being impregnated by the Holy Spirit through her ears. "[Some], who found it difficult to believe that even God could impregnate the Blessed Mary without her losing her virginity, developed the idea that she was impregnated through the ear by the Archangel Gabriel, or by God Himself" (G. Rattray Taylor, *Sex in History* [New York: Harper Torchbooks, 1970], 61–62).

7. Henry van Dyke, "Hymn of Joy," in *The Poems of Henry Van Dyke*, rev. ed. (New York: Charles Scribner's Sons, 1920), 232–33; quotation on 233.The metaphor of the "morning stars" (as in "The morning stars sang together") comes from Job 38:7.

8. A version of this ballad appears in John A. Lomax, *American Ballads and Folksongs* (New York: Macmillan, 1941), 601.

9. David Hempton, *Methodism: Empire of the Spirit* (New Haven, Conn.: Yale University Press, 2005), 56.

10. This is Nathan Hatch's phrase in "The Puzzle of American Methodism," in *American Church History: A Reader*, ed. Henry Warner Bowden and P. C. Kemeny (Nashville: Abingdon, 1998), 288.

11. Ibid.

12. 1 Corinthians 14:10.

13. John Wesley, preface to *Primitive Physic; or, An Easy and Natural Method of Curing Most Diseases. To Which Is Added the General Receipt Book Containing Upwards of Four Hundred of the Most Useful and Valuable Receipts* (London: Barr, 1843), iii.

14. This connection was made explicit in William Tyndale's 1525 translation of the Bible from Greek into English: *The Newe Testament*, trans. William Tyndale (1525; repr., London: D. Paladine Developments, 1976), fol. lxxiiii. See also Leonard Sweet, *The Jesus Prescription for a Healthy Life* (Nashville: Abingdon, 1996), 12.

15. Maltbie D. Babcock, "This Is My Father's World" (1901), *The United Methodist Hymnal* (Nashville: The United Methodist Publishing House, 1989), 144.

16. Fanny Crosby, "Rescue the Perishing" (1869), *The United Methodist Hymnal* (Nashville: The United Methodist Publishing House, 1989), 591.

17. Harry Mark Petrakis, *A Dream of Kings* (New York: David McKay, 1966), 3.

18. Ibid., 3–4.

19. Malachi 4:2.

20. Charles Wesley, "Hark! the Herald Angels Sing," *The United Methodist Hymnal* (Nashville: The United Methodist Publishing House, 1989), 240.

21. Crosby, "Rescue the Perishing," 591.

22. John Wesley, preface to *A Collection of Hymns for the Use of the People Called Methodists* (1780), ed. Franz Hildebrandt, Oliver A. Beckerlegge, and James Dale, vol. 7 of *The Works of John Wesley* (Nashville: Abingdon, 1983), 74.

23. Quoted in the memorial tribute to Charles Wesley, "Annual Minutes of Some Late Conversations, 1788, London, Tuesday July 29, 1788," in *The Methodist Societies: The Minutes of Conference*, ed. Henry D. Rack, vol. 10 of *The Works of John Wesley* (Nashville: Abingdon, 2011), 646.

24. This point is made in Shannon Steed Sigler's essay "Exploring the Vocation of the Wesleyan Artist," *SEEN: The Journal of CIVA, Christians in the Visual Arts* 8, no. 2 (2008), http://www.bu.edu/cpt/files/2010/04/WesleyanAestheticArticle.pdf.

25. Felix Mendelssohn, "To Marc-André Souchay, 15 October 1842," in *Music and Aesthetics in the Eighteenth and Early Nineteenth Centuries*, ed. Peter Le Huray and James Day (Cambridge, UK: Cambridge University Press, 1981), 457.

26. Romans 7:22; 8:10; 2 Corinthians 4:16.

27. Jonathan Edwards, [A letter to Sir William Pepperell, the Governor of Massachusetts], Stockbridge, Nov. 28, 1751, in *The Works of President Edwards: With a Memoir of His Life* (New York: G. & C. & H. Carvill, 1830), 1:478.

28. Revelation 19:6.

29. Charles Wesley, "O For a Thousand Tongues to Sing" (1739), *The United Methodist Hymnal* (Nashville: The United Methodist Publishing House, 1989), 57.

30. Thanks to Tom Albin, Dean of the Upper Room Chapel, Nashville, for providing this verifying this information.

31. J. M. Synge, *The Aron Islands*, with drawings by Jack B. Yeats (Boston: John W. Luce, 1911), 181.

32. For references to "listening multitude," in John Wesley, *Journals and Diaries*, ed. W. Reginald Ward and Richard P. Heitzenrater, vols. 20–24 of *The Works of John Wesley* (Nashville: Abingdon, 1991–2003), see Lifton

near Launceston, Friday, September 16, 1748: "We took a horse and came in the evening to Lifton near Launceston. One who removed from Camelford hither received us gladly. I had not been well all day, so was not sorry they had had no notice of my coming. Being much better in the morning, I preached at seven in the street to a listening multitude, on 'Repent ye and believe the gospel'" (*Journals and Diaries* 3:248 [*Works* 20, 1991]); St. Just, Saturday, September 7, 1751: "I rode in a stormy afternoon to St. Just. But the rain would not let me preach abroad either that evening or on Sunday morning. About noon I made shift to stand on the lee side of an house in Morah and preach Christ to a listening multitude" (*Journals and Diaries* 3:401 [*Works* 20, 1991]); Stockton, Tuesday, April 28, 1752: "It rained all the way to Stockton, but was fair all the time I stood in the main street and explained to a listening multitude the 'joy' that is in heaven over one sinner that repenteth'" (*Journals and Diaries* 3:422 [*Works* 20, 1991]); Cockermouth, Whit Sunday, May 29, 1757: "After preaching at eight and at two I hastened to Cockermouth. I began without delay and cried to the listening multitude, 'If any man thirst, let him come unto me and drink.' The word had free course. Even the gentry desired to drink of the 'living water'" (*Journals and Diaries* 4:104 [*Works* 21, 1992]); Epworth, Friday, July 15, 1757: "Before seven I reached Epworth and preached in the market-place to a listening multitude" (*Journals and Diaries* 4:114 [*Works* 21, 1992]); Bandon, Ireland, Tuesday, July 11, 1758: "I rode with James Morgan to Bandon and preached in the market-house to a listening multitude" (*Journals and Diaries* 4:158 [*Works* 21, 1992]); Alkborough, Friday, April 13, 1759: "Having appointed to preach at Alkborough at one, I set out between seven and eight. I was in hopes of coming thither before church began, but I did not consider the Lincolnshire roads. With some difficulty we reached it before noon and found there was no service at the church. I preached in the churchyard at one to a listening multitude—most of whom, I suppose, had never heard this kind of preaching before. Many of them were in tears and pressed after me into the house where we met the society. I could not but hope that some of these will press into the kingdom of heaven" (*Journals and Diaries* 4:183 [*Works* 21, 1992]); Shields, Monday, May 25, 1761: "I rode to Shields and preached in an open place to a listening multitude. Many of them followed me to South Shields, where I preached in the evening to almost double the congregation. How ripe for the gospel are these also! What is wanting but more labourers?" (*Journals and Diaries* 4:325 [*Works* 21, 1992]); Gateshead, Sunday, May 20, 1764: "Between eight and nine, I preached in Gateshead to a listening multitude. I believe their number was doubled at the Fell, about two in the afternoon" (*Journals and Diaries* 4:465 [*Works* 21, 1992]); Kingswood, Sunday, March 16, 1766: "I preached in Princes Street at eight on 'Awakke, thou that sleepest', and at the Square [King Square] in the evening, to a listening multitude, on 'Come, Lord Jesus!" (*Journals and Diaries* 5:32 [*Works* 22, 1993]); St. Ives(?), Thursday, September 1, 1768: "The grass being wet, we could not stand in the meadow, but we found an open space, where I called a listening multitude to return to him who 'hath' not 'forgotten to be gracious'" (*Journals and Diaries* 5:156 [*Works* 22, 1993]); Cockhill, Sunday, April 16, 1769: "At nine, I preached in a meadow near Cockhill to a listening multitude. I suppose we should have had twice the number in the evening, but the rain prevented. The grass being wet, I stood in the highway while many stood in the neighbouring houses. And the Word of God was as the rain upon the tender herb" (*Journals and Diaries* 5:178 [*Works* 22, 1993]); Chatham, Monday, December 4, 1769: "I went to Chatham. Mr. Whitefield's people (so called) refusing me the use of their room, I preached in the barracks to a listening multitude, and our hearts were sweetly enlarged and knit together. One of their society, grieved at the bigotry of his brethren, invited me to prach in the house in the morning, which I did (the barracks not being open) to as many as it could well contain" (*Journals and Diaries* 5:211 [*Works* 22, 1993]); Clonmel, Ireland, Monday, April 29, 1771: "In the evening, I preached in the market-place at Clonmel to a listening multitude. Some seemed inclined to disturb, but the serious, well behaved troopers kept them all in awe" (*Journals and Diaries* 5:271 [*Works* 22, 1993]); Tadcaster, Sunday, July 10, 1774: "Some of Tadcaster informing me that the minister was willing I should preach in the church, I went thither in the morning. But his mind was changed. So I preached in the street to a listening multitude from the Lesson for the Day on the 'righteousness' which 'exceeds that of the Scribes and Pharisees'" (*Journals and Diaries* 5:420 [*Works* 22, 1993]); Penzance, September 1, 1774: "In the evening, I took my stand at the end of the town and preached the whole gospel to a listening multitude. I then earnestly exhorted the society to 'follow after peace and holiness'" (*Journals and Diaries* 5:427 [*Works* 22, 1993]); he writes prior to the above: "When the people here were as roaring lions we had all the ground to ourselves. Now they are become lambs. Mr. S____h and his friends step in and take true pains to make a rent in the society" (*Journals and Diaries* 5:427 [*Works* 22, 1993]); Manchester, Thursday, April 4, 1776: "On Easter Day the preaching-house at Manchester contained the congregation pretty well at seven in the morning. But in the afternooon, I was obliged to be abroad, thousands upon thousands flocking together. I stood in a convenient place, almost over against the Infirmary, and exhorted a listening multitude to 'live unto him who died for them and rose again'" (*Journals and Diaries* 6:8 [*Works* 23, 1995]); Banff, Monday, May 20, 1776: "I preached about eleven at Oldmeldrum, but could not reach Banff till near seven in the evening. I went directly to the parade and proclaimed to a listening multitude, 'The grace of our Lord Jesus Christ.' All behaved well but a few gentry, whom I rebuked openly. And they stood corrected" ["Banff is one of the neatest and most elegant towns that I have seen in Scotland"] (*Journals and Diaries* 6:15 [*Works* 23, 1995]); Frome, Wednesday, September 11, 1776: "I preached about one at Bath, and about six, in a meadow near the preaching-house in Frome, besought a listening multitude 'not to receive the grace of God in vain'" (*Journals and Diaries* 6:33 [*Works* 23, 1995]); Thorne, Thursday, June 8, 1780: "I preached on the Green at Throne to a listening multitude. Only two or three were much *diverted* at the thought of 'seeing the dead, small and great standing before God!'" (*Journals and Diaries* 6:175 [*Works* 23,

1995]); Bristol, Sunday, March 18, 1787: "preached her ["Sarah Bulgin, went to rest in the full triumph of faith" the Wednesday before] funeral sermon to a listening multitude and had such a number of communicants as was never seen gather at Bristol room before" (*Journals and Diaries* 7:8 [*Works* 24, 2003]); Bandon, Thursday, May 10, 1787: "In the evening, finding no building would contain the congregation, I stood in the main street and testified to a listening multitude, 'This is not your rest.' I then administered the Lord's Supper to the society, and God gave us a remarkable blessing" (*Journals and Diaries* 7:24 [*Works* 24, 2003]); Armagh, Ireland, Monday, June 18, 1787: "In the evening, I preached once more in Mr. M'Geough's avenue, and a listening multitude seriously attended. Surely there will be a harvest here also by and by, although hitherto we see but little fruit" (*Journals and Diaries* 7:39 [*Works* 24, 2003]); Epworth, Sunday, July 6, 1788: "At four, I preached in the market-place on Rom. 6:23 and vehemently exhorted the listening multitude to choose the better part" (*Journals and Diaries* 7:101 [*Works* 24, 2003]).

33. Charles Wesley was only doing what the Apostle Paul had done before him: he got people to sing theology. The first theological hymn was "The Christ Hymn," where Paul incorporates into the Letter to the Philippians an early hymn, a *carmina Christi*, which sings the kenotic theology of the cross and summons disciples not to imitate Christ, which would be humanly impossible, but to live in the identity of who they are in Christ. See Philippians 2:6-11. The Apostle Paul instructed the Colossians, "Let the word of Christ dwell in you richly; teach and admonish one another in all wisdom; and with gratitude in your hearts sing psalms, hymns, and spiritual songs to God. And whatever you do, in word or deed, do everything in the name of the Lord Jesus, giving thanks to God the Father through him" (Colossians 3:16-17).

34. John 12:20-32.

35. Orange Scott, *The New and Improved Camp Meeting Hymn Book: Being a Choice Selection of Hymns from the Most Approved Authors*, 2nd ed. (Brookfield, Mass.: The Compiler; printed by E. and G. Merriam, 1831), iii.

36. Babcock, "This Is My Father's World" (1901).

37. Hempton, *Methodism*, 56.

38. As quoted in Winthrop S. Hudson, "Shouting Methodist" *Encounter* 29 (Winter 1968): 73 (73-84). This is identified as being from *The Chorus*, comp. A. S. Jenks and D. Gilkey (Philadelphia, 1860).

39. As quoted in Charles A. Johnson, *The Frontier Camp Meeting: Religion's Harvest Time* (Dallas: Southern Methodist University Press, 1955), 204; Stith Mead, *A General Selection of the Newest and Most Admired Hymns and Spiritual Songs Now in Use* (Richmond: Printed by Seaton Grantland, 1807), 79.

40. This version appears as the third stanza in a compilation of songs by the Methodist Episcopal minister David B. Mintz, *Spiritual Song Book: Designed as an Assistant for the Pious of All Denominations* (Halifax, N.C.: Abraham Hodge, 1805); as recorded in George P. Jackson, *White and Negro Spirituals: Their Life Span and Kinship* (New York: J. J. Augustin, 1943), 56.

41. As quoted in Johnson, *The Frontier Camp Meeting*, 233; Alexander Campbell, "Aspects of Methodism," *Millennial Harbinger* (Bethany, Va.) 7 (August 1843): 365. For the Wesleys' experiences with manifestations, see Steve Beard, *John Wesley and the "Toronto" Blessing* (Wilmore, KY: Thunderstruck Communications, 1996), in which he has a section on the Holy Laugh. John and Charles both experience uncontrolled laughter while walking (as quoted by John in "A Letter to the Right Reverend the Lord Bishop of Gloucester: Occasioned by His Tract, On the Office and Operations of the Holy Spirit," in *The Appeals to Men of Reason and Religion and Certain Related Open Letters*, ed. Gerald R. Cragg [Oxford: Clarendon Press, 1975], 469), and Methodist meetings often were engulfed in laughter.

42. Quoted in *Esquire* 98 (1982): viii.

43. As quoted in Hudson, "Shouting Methodist," 74.

44. As quoted in Johnson, *The Frontier Camp Meeting*, 262-64. Johnson identifies this dialogue song as being from *The Hesperian Harp*, compiled by William Hauser, printed in Philadelphia, 1848, and reprinted in George P. Jackson, ed., *Down-East Spirituals and Others* (New York, 1939), 13-15. Johnson adds: "Two sections of the camp meeting audience sang these verses alternately. The practice of seating the women on one side and the men on the other seemed to have furthered the use of this dramatic type of song" (262).

45. Hudson, "Shouting Methodist."

46. John Wesley, "Directions for Singing," as quoted in *The United Methodist Hymnal* (Nashville: The United Methodist Publishing House, 1989), vii.

47. Romans 10:17 NKJV.

48. Charles Wesley, "Jesus, Lover of My Soul," *The United Methodist Hymnal* (Nashville: The United Methodist Publishing House, 1989), 479.

49. "Charm of the Butter," in Carmina Gadelica: Hymns and Incantations with Illustrative Notes on Words, Rites, and Customs, Dying and Obsolete: Orally Collected in the Highlands and Islands of Scotland, ed. Alexander Carmichael (Edinburgh: Scottish Academic Press, 1978), 4:85.

50. See Winthrop S. Hudson, "The Methodist Age in America," *Methodist History* 12 (April 1974): 3-15. Also see David Martin, *Tongues of Fire: The Explosion of Protestantism in Latin America* (Cambridge, Mass.: Basil Blackwell, 1990), 21: "Arminian evangelical Protestantism provides the *differentia specifica* of the American religious and cultural ethos. . . . The whole American style was and is 'Methodist' in its emphases," insisting on openness and sincerity rather than form and privacy. For these reasons, Hudson, Martin, and Hatch agree that, contrary to Europe, in America, because of Methodism, "popular culture remained more religious than did high culture." See Nathan O. Hatch, "The Puzzle of American Method-

ism," in *Methodism and the Shaping of American Culture*, ed. John Wigger and Nathan O. Hatch (Nashville: Kingswood, 2001), 37–38.

51. Acts 2:2-3 NKJV.

52. For those with Calvinist sounds, see George Whitefield or, more recently, Dr. Martyn Lloyd-Jones of the "Welsh Calvinistic Methodist Church." For information about Lloyd-Jones, see "Dr. Martyn Lloyd-Jones Online," http://www.misterrichardson.com/mlj.html.

53. Frank Kermode makes this point.

54. See the preview on YouTube, "An Idea Can Transform the World—Inception Movie," http://www.youtube.com/watch?v=8Uahq8Nt9Y0.

55. See Craig Bubeck's Reformed approach to holiness called "No Stinking Up God's Place! (or, 'How to Be Perfect Like God')", *The Internet Monk*, October 7, 2011, http://www.internetmonk.com/archive/no-stinking-up-god%E2%80%99s-place-or-%E2%80%9Chow-to-be-perfect-like-god%E2%80%9D.

56. Judith Maizel-Long, "Theology Sung and Celebrated," in *Unmasking Methodist Theology*, ed. Clive Marsh, Brian Beck, Angela Shier-Jones, and Helen Wareing (New York: Continuum, 2004), 51.

57. Gustave Flaubert, *"À Madame Tennant, jour de Noël 1876,"* in *Correspondance 1871–1877*, Oeuvres Complètes 15 (Paris: Club de l'Honnête Homme, 1975), 516.

58. SanDee Whitfield Tillee, *Lord, I've Been in Hell So Long* (Nashville: Upper Room Book, 1978).

59. My favorite line from Hans Christian Andersen's "The Snow Queen" (1845), in *Hans Andersen's Fairy Tales* (Boston: DeWolfe, Fiske, 1898), 90, is: "It is no use asking the flowers; they know only their own songs, and can give me no information."

60. See Joseph D. McPherson, *"Our People Die Well": Glorious Accounts of Early Methodists at Death's Door* (Bloomington, Ind.: AuthorHouse, 2008).

61. As quoted in Thomas Karshan, *Vladimir Nabokov and the Art of Play* (New York: Oxford University Press, 2011).

62. Max Weber, *The Protestant Ethic and the Spirit of Capitalism*, trans. Talcott Parsons (New York: Charles Scribner's Sons, 1948).

63. Tim Dowley, *Christian Music: A Global History* (Minneapolis: Augsburg Fortress Press, 2011), 118.

64. A paraphrase of Philippians 4:6.

65. 1 Timothy 4:4 NIV.

66. Dorothy Sayers once said that Jesus' friends have done to him what his enemies would never have dreamed of doing. She writes: "This is the dogma we find so dull—this terrifying drama of which God is the victim and hero. . . . We have very efficiently pared the claws of the Lion of Judah, certified Him 'meek and mild,' and recommended Him as a fitting household pet for pale curates and pious old ladies. . . . He was emphatically not a dull man in His human lifetime, and if He was God, there can be nothing dull about God." See Sayers, "The Greatest Drama Ever Staged," in *Creed or Chaos* (New York: Harcourt, Brace, 1949), 5–6.

67. John Wesley, footnote on 2 Peter 1:7, *Explanatory Notes Upon the New Testament* (Grand Rapids, Mich.: Baker, 1981), 2. The full quote is "No sullenness, sternness, moroseness: 'Sour godliness,' so called is of the devil."

68. W. E. Sangster, "You Can't Make People Good," in *Can I Know God? and Other Sermons* (New York: Abingdon, 1960), 156.

69. Psalm 126:2-3 NIV.

70. The context of this quote is different from this discussion. See the letter "To the Rev. Francis Asbury, London, September 20, 1788," as found in *The Works of the Reverend John Wesley: First American Complete and Standard Edition from the Latest London Edition, with the Last Corrections of the Author: Comprehending Also Numerous Translations, Notes, and an Original Preface, etc.*, by John Emory (New York: J. Emory and B. Waugh, 1831), 7:188.

71. Isaac Watts, "Joy to the World," and "Come Ye That Love the Lord," in Cyprian T. Rust, *Break of Day in the Eighteenth Century: A History and a Specimen of Its First Book of English Sacred Song: 300 Hymns of Dr. Watts, Carefully Selected and Arranged, with a Sketch of Their History* (London: William Hunt, 1880), 59, 134.

72. John Wesley, "The Character of a Methodist," in *The Methodist Societies: History, Nature, and Design*, ed. Rupert E. Davies, vol. 9 of *The Works of John Wesley* (Nashville: Abingdon, 1989), 35.

73. Watts, "Joy to the World," 59.

74. Nehemiah 8:10 NIV.

75. You can find a version of this story in Colin Morris, introduction to *Bugles in the Afternoon* (Philadelphia: Westminster, 1977), 9.

76. John Wesley, "The Unity of the Divine Being" [Dublin: April 9, 1789], in *Sermons*, ed. Albert C. Outler, vol. 4 of *The Works of John Wesley* (Nashville: Abingdon, 1987), 64.

77. Psalm 16:11.

78. Wesley, "The Unity of the Divine Being," 66–67.

79. C. S. Lewis, *Letters to Malcolm: Chiefly on Prayer* (New York: Harcourt, Brace & World, 1964), 93.

80. Pat Riley, "The Winner Within's Ladder of Evolution," in *The Winner Within: A Life Plan for Team Players* (New York: Putnam's Sons, 1993), 251.

81. Simone Weil, *Gravity and Grace*, trans. Emma Crawford and Mario von der Ruhr (New York: Rutledge, 2002), 34.

82. Loyal Jones, "Buell Kazee," biographical notes to LP album *Buell Kazee* (Whitesburg, Ky: June Appal Recordings, 1978).

83. Buell Kazee, *Faith Is the Victory* (Grand Rapids, Mich.:Eerdmans, 1951), 174–75.

84. Ibid., 180.

85. Romans 7:17.

86. The best book on the subject is by Vander Meer, *Recovering from Churchism: How to Renew, Grow, and Celebrate Your Church* (Grand Rapids, Mich.: Edenridge Press, 2011).

87. Romans 12:2 NIV.

88. Mark Vernon, "Incredible Views," *TLS: Times Literary Supplement* (April 2, 2010): 8–9, http://www.templeton-cambridge.org/fellows/showarticle.php?article=396.

89. For more on followership, see Leonard Sweet, *I Am a Follower: The Way, Truth, and Life of Following Jesus* (Nashville: Thomas Nelson, forthcoming).

90. Revelation 21:5.

91. Habakkuk 2:20.

92. Richard Kostelanetz, *Conversing with Cage*, 2nd ed. (New York: Routledge, 2003), 189.

93. For more, see, for example, Larry J. Solomon, "The Sounds of Silence: John Cage and 4'33", http://solomonsmusic.net/4min33se.htm.

94. Rollo May, *Freedom and Destiny* (New York: Norton, 1981), 165.

95. For more on this, see Rollo May, "The Significance of the Pause," in *Freedom and Destiny* (New York: Norton, 1981), 163–84.

96. Clara H. Scott, "Open My Eyes, That I May See," *The United Methodist Hymnal* (Nashville: The United Methodist Publishing House, 1989), 454.

97. Quoted in Peter Hebblethwaite, *Pope John Paul II and the Church* (Kansas City, Mo.: Sheed & Ward, 1995), 287.

98. John Wesley, "Notes on St. Paul's First Epistle to the Thessalonians [ch. 5: verse 16]," in *Explanatory Notes Upon the New Testament: Romans to Revelation* (Grand Rapids, MI: Baker Book).

99. John Wesley, "Notes on St. Paul's Epistle to the Ephesians [ch. 6: verse 18]," *Explanatory Notes Upon the New Testament*.

100. Cf. Acts 2:42.

101. See John Wesley's 1744 "An Earnest Appeal to Men of Reason and Religion," in Cragg, *The Appeals to Men*, 45-94.

102. Prayer bumps or prayer scars are "raisins" on the forehead (*zabiba/zebiba/zebibah* in Arabic) that form from the friction generated by the contact of the forehead with the prayer mat or floor. Sometimes the prayer bump is simply discolored skin and a thick callus.

103. Martin Luther, *Lectures on Romans*, ed. Hilton C. Oswald, vol. 25 of *Luther's Works* (Saint Louis: Concordia, 1092), 390.

104. John Wesley, "A Collection of Forms of Prayer for Everyday in the Week," in Emory, *The Works of the Reverend John Wesley*, 7:558. See also Ole E. Borgan, "John Wesley: Sacramental Theology: No Ends Without the Means," in *Contemporary Perspectives*, ed. John Stacey (London: Epworth Press, 1988), 73: "The four parts of all prayers: deprecation (pleading for forgiveness and mercy), petition (asking), intercession (praying for others) and thanksgiving. Prayer prepares and enables him who prays to receive God's blessings."

105. John Bunyan, *I Will Pray with the Spirit, in His Doctrine of the Law and Grace Unfolded and I Will Pray with the Spirit*, ed. Richard L. Greaves (Oxford: Clarendon, 1976), 258.

106. Johann Wolfgang von Goethe, *William Meister's Travels: or The Renunciants: A Novel*, in *Goethe's Wilhelm Meister's Apprenticeship and Travels*, trans. Thomas Carlyle, ed. Clement King Shorter (Chicago: A. C. McClurg, 1890), 2:220.

107. Graeme Wood, "The Fortunate Ones," *Atlantic* (April 2011): 80.

108. Romans 7:15.

109. See Mark 8:33; Luke 24:25; and John 14:9.

2. The Song of Fire

1. Susan Goldin-Meadow of the University of Chicago is the one who conducted the studies. See "A Handwaving Approach to Arithmetic," *Economist* (February 21, 2009): 80.

2. Heather Stas and C. Bottomley, "Josh Groban: Don't Call Him Diva (Except in the Shower)," November 26, 2003, VH1.com, http://www.vh1.com/artists/interview/1480820/11262003/groban_josh.jhtml.

3. Richard Collier, *The General Next to God: The Story of William Booth and the Salvation Army* (New York: Dutton 1965), 146.

4. William Butler Yeats, "The Second Coming," in *The Collected Poems of W. B. Yeats*, rev. 2nd ed., ed. Richard J. Finneran (New York: Scribner Paperback Poetry, 1989), 187.

5. John Robert Seeley, *Ecce Homo: A Survey of the Life and Work of Jesus Christ*, new ed. (London: Macmillan, 1867), 7.

6. J. Maurus, *Use Your Stress to Keep Away Distress*, rev. ed. (Mumbai, India: Better Yourself Books, 2005), 57.

7. Chuck Gallozzi states this in "Developing Passion," *Personal-Development.com*, http://www.person al-development.com/chuck/passion.htm.

8. Thomas Chalmers, "The Importance of Civil Government to Society," in *Discourses on the Application of Christianity to the Commercial and Ordinary Affairs of Life*, vol. 6 of *The Works of Thomas Chalmers* (New York: Robert Carter, 1840), 359.

9. See Jaroslav Pelikan, *Christian Doctrine and Modern Culture (Since 1700)*, vol. 5 of *The Christian Tradition: A History of the Development of Doctrine* (Chicago: University of Chicago Press, 1989), 132. See also John Wesley, "Upon Our Lord's Sermon on the Mount, Discourse the Eleventh," in his *Sermons*, ed. Albert C. Outler, vol. 1 of *The Works of John Wesley* (Nashville: Abingdon, 1984), 1:672–73.

10. This is a story that appears with many variations and in a variety of sources. For one version where a mule is the butt of the joke, see California Land Title Association, *Proceedings of the Annual Convention*, 48 (1958): 11.

11. The first quote is from Augustus Toplady, "An Old Fox Tarred and Feathered: Occasioned by What Is Called Mr. John Wesley's Calm Address to Our American Colonies," in *The Works of Augustus Toplady, A.B.* (London: Printed for the Proprietors, 1794), 5:450. The second quote, also from Toplady, "A Letter to the Rev. Mr. Wesley, Relative to His Abridgment of Zanchius on Predestination," in ibid., 5:343. For a transcript of the talk, see John Betjeman, "Augustus Toplady," Sunday 23 June 1946, in his *Trains and Buttered Toast: Selected Radio Talks*, ed. Stephen Games (London: John Murray, 2006), 196–203.

12. John Betjeman, *Trains and Buttered Toast: Selected Radio Talks*, ed. Stephen Games (2006).

13. A Methodist's dictum is not "Let Not Your Hearts Be Troubled," but "Let Something You Dismay." At least their heads ought to be troubled and dismayed.

14. For one example of "be electrified daily," see the letter to Samuel Bradburn, March 13, 1788, in *The Letters of the Rev. John Wesley, A.M.*, ed. John Telford (London: Epworth Press, 1931) 8:45. See also *The Desideratum: or Electricity Made Plain and Useful* (Nashville: Abingdon, 1992 (first published 1759). See also his *Primitive Physic*, with an introd. by A. Wesley Hill (London: Epworth Press, 1960, first published 1747). Electronconvulsive therapy (ECT), or what is popularly known today as "shock therapy," fell into disrepute until the late 1990s. For failed applications that partially doomed it, consider the ECT of Ernest Hemingway and Sylvia Plath, both of whom subsequently committed suicide.

15. Character is an inside-out affair. Context is an outside-in dynamic. For more on this, see Leonard Sweet, *Jesus Drives Me Crazy* (Grand Rapids, Mich.: Zondervan, 2003).

16. John Wesley, Entry for May 24, 1738, *Journal and Diaries,* ed. W. Reginald Ward and Richard P. Heitzenrater The Works of John Wesley, 18, (Nashville: Abingdon, 1988) 1:249-50.

17. Charles Wesley, entry for Sunday, May 21, 1738, *The Journal of Charles Wesley* (Grand Rapids, Mich.: Baker Book House, 1980), 1:91–92.

18. J. Bruce Behney and Paul H. Eller, *The History of the Evangelical United Brethren Church*, ed. Kenneth W. Krueger (Nashville: Abingdon, 1979), 35–36.

19. Raymond W. Albright, *A History of the Evangelical Church* (Harrisburg, PA: The Evangelical Press, 1945), 35.

20. As referenced in Anthony De Mello, *The Song of the Bird* (Garden City, N.Y.: Image, 1984), 130.

21. In the same letter, Briggs complained that he could not find "that *deep union* with you as I have with some." "From William Briggs, London April 5, 1750," in *Letters II, 1750–1755*, ed. Frank Baker, vol. 26 of *The Works of John Wesley* (Oxford: Clarendon, 1982), 415. Thanks to John Kent, *Wesley and the Wesleyans* (Cambridge: Cambridge University Press, 2002), 196, for this reference, although the actual one is somewhat different from that cited by Kent.

22. John Wesley, "Saturday, February 7, [1736]," Ward and Heitzenrater, *Journals and Diaries*, 1:145–46.

23. Thomas Traherne, *A Sober View of Dr. Twisses His Considerations*, in *The Works of Thomas Traherne*, ed. Jan Ross (Rochester, NY: D. S. Brewer, 2005), I:79, 195.

24. Dr. Martin Luther's Commentary upon the Epistle to the Galatians, abridged, without any Alterations . . . (London: Printed for J. Brotherton, 1734), 72.

25. Charles Wesley, "God of Almighty Love," *A Collection of Hymns for the Use of the People Called Methodists* (1780), ed. Franz Hildebrandt, Oliver A. Beckerlegge, and James Dale, vol. 7 of *The Works of John Wesley* (Nashville: Abingdon, 1983), 469. Thanks to Margaret Jones, "Growing in Grace and Holiness," in *Unmasking Methodist Theology: A Way Forward* (New York: Continuum, 2004), for reminding me of this hymn.

26. Myron S. Augsburger, *The Peacemaker* (Nashville: Abingdon, 1987), 203.

27. Charles Wesley, "A Charge to Keep I Have," *The United Methodist Hymnal: Book of United Methodist Worship* (Nashville: The United Methodist Publishing House, 1989), 413.

28. See my introduction: "Garden, Park, Glen, Meadow, in *The Church in the Emerging Culture: Five Perspectives*, ed. Leonard Sweet (Grand Rapids, MI: Zondervan, 2003), 13–41.

29. For more on this, see my *Viral: How Social Networking Is Poised to Ignite Revival* (Colorado Springs, Colo.: WaterBrook, 2012).

30. For more on this last question, see Joseph R. Myers, *The Search to Belong* (Grand Rapids, Mich.: Zondervan, 2003); and Myers, *The Gospel According to Starbucks: Living with a Grande Passion* (Colorado Springs, Colo.: WaterBrook, 2007).

31. Jacob Albright, as quoted in Raymond W. Albright, *A History of the Evangelical Church*, 40.

32. See W. Stephen Gunter and Elaine Robinson, eds., *Considering the Great Commission: Evangelism and Mission in the Wesleyan Spirit* (Nashville: Abingdon, 2005); and Rick Shrout, *Street-Crossers: Conversations with Simple Church Planters and Stories of Those Who Send Them* (Eugene, Ore.: Wipf & Stock, 2011).

33. Wendell Berry, foreword to *Scripture, Culture, and Agriculture: An Agrarian Reading of the Bible*, ed. Ellen F. Davis (Cambridge: Cambridge University Press, 2009), xiii.

34. Jonathan Swift, "To M. Pope, September 29, 1725," in *The Works of Jonathan Swift: Containing Interesting and Valuable Papers, Not Hitherto Published* (London: Henry G. Bohn, 1843), 2:579.

35. As quoted by Michael Scammell, *Koestler: The Literary and Political Odyssey* (New York: Random House, 2009), 447.

36. Shrout, *Street-Crossers*, xv.

37. As quoted by Ruth Rouse, *A History of the Ecumenical Movement, 1517-1948*, 4th ed., ed. Ruth Rouse and Stephen Charles Neill (Geneva, Switzerland: World Council of Churches, 1993), 287.

38. Jews are called "Jews" because they come from Judea. For more on the New Testament church, see Nee Duo-Sheng ("Watchman Nee") of China, in his book *Concerning Our Missions* (London: Witness and Testimony Society, 1939).

39. See Sweet, *Viral*.

40. See Jesus in John 17.

41. "He put a new song in my mouth" (Psalm 40:3).

42. Shortly after his conversion, Jacob Albright began to hear God calling him to be an itinerant evangelist among his Pennsylvania neighbors. Plagued with many doubts, he wrote, "By contending with these doubts, I became more and more, and finally, fully convinced that God had called me to the great work of proclaiming his Word and gospel." Raymond W. Albright, *A History of the Evangelical Church*, 41.

3. The Song of Wind

1. "Where two or three are gathered together in my name, there am I in the midst of them."

2. For Otterbein's early class meetings, see Bruce Behney and Paul H. Eller, *The History of the Evangelical United Brethren Church*, ed. Kenneth W. Krueger (Nashville: Abingdon Press, 1979), 48. For Albright's early class meetings, see Raymond W. Albright, *A History of the Evangelical Church* (Harrisburg, PA: Evangelical Press, 1945), 66.

3. See John Kent, *Wesley and the Wesleyans: Religion in Eighteenth-Century Britain* (New York: Cambridge University Press, 2002), 216n27.

4. As cited by Ian Bradley in "Notes of Discord," *Tablet* (July 16, 2011): 23.

5. For more on this, see Ray Sherman Anderson, *Spiritual Caregiving as Secular Sacrament: A Critical Theology for Professional Caregivers* (New York: J. Kingsley, 2003), 71–72.

6. From the title of Edna St. Vincent Millay, *"There Are No Islands, Any More": Lines Written in Passion and in Deep Concern for England, France and My Own Country* (New York: Harper, 1940).

7. I thank Craig Oldenburg for this story.

8. Heikki Räisänen, *The Rise of Christian Beliefs: The Thought World of Early Christians* (Minneapolis: Fortress, 2009).

9. Luke 15:2, paraphrased.

10. Angela Shier-Jones, "Being Methodical: Theology within Church Structures," in *Unmasking Methodist Theology: A Way Forward*, ed. Clive Marsh, Brian Beck, Angela Shier-Jones, and Helen Waring (New York: Continuum, 2004), 29.

11. Andrew C. Thompson, "Discipleship: Christian Life and The Means of Grace," in *Generation Rising: Future with Hope for The United Methodist Church*, ed. Andrew C. Thompson (Nashville: Abingdon, 2011), 6.

12. Gordon G. Johnson, *My Church: A Manual of Baptist Faith and Action* (Chicago: Harvest Publications, 1963), 88.

13. John 20:21.

14. Mark 16:15 NIV, italics added.

15. Thomas Aquinas, *Summa Contra Gentiles*, trans. A. C. Pegis (Notre Dame, IN: University of Notre Dame Press, 1975), 1:67.

16. "From the Revd. William Law, May 19, 1738," in *Letters*, ed. Frank Baker, vol. 25 of *The Works of John Wesley* (Oxford: Clarendon Press, 1980), 1:545.

17. Samuel Johnson, "Hester Thrale, Thursday 19 June 1783," in *The Letters of Samuel Johnson*, ed. Bruce Redford (Princeton, NJ: Princeton University Press, 1994), 4:151n6.

18. G. W. F. Hegel, *Lectures on the Philosophy of Religion*, ed. Peter C. Hodgson, trans. R. F. Brown, P. C. Hodgson, and J. M. Stewart (Berkeley: University of California Press, 1984), 1:258.

19. This "tweezers" metaphor and the Hegel quote come from Nicholas Lash, *Holiness, Speech and Silence: Reflections on the Question of God* (Burlington, Vt.: Ashgate, 2004), 85.

20. For a full discussion, see "A Letter to the Right Reverend the Lord Bishop of Gloucester: Occasioned by His Tract 'On the Office and Operations of the Holy Spirit,'" November 26, 1762, in *The Works of the Reverend John Wesley*, ed. John Emory (New York: B. Waugh and T. Mason, 1835), 443–80.

21. See, for example, Robert Kirk, *Zombies and Consciousness* (New York: Oxford University Press, 2007).

22. Stephen Eric Bronner, *Reclaiming the Enlightenment: Toward a Politics of Radical Engagement* (New York: Columbia University Press, 2004), 167.

23. It contains only one brief paragraph in 250 pages devoted to climate change. See Pontifical Council for Justice and Peace, *Compendium of the Social Doctrine of the Church*, paragraph 470 (Washington, D.C.: United States Conference of Catholic bishops, 2004), 37, http://www.vatican.va/roman_curia/pontifical_councils/justpeace/documents/rc_pc_justpeace_doc_20060526_compendio-dott-soc_en.html.

24. So argued William B. Fitzgerald, *The Roots of Methodism* (London: Epworth Press, 1903), 173.

25. Charles Darwin, *On the Origin of Species: A Facsimile of the First Edition*, intro. Ernst Mayr (Cambridge, Mass.: Harvard University Press, 1966), 489.

26. Charles Wesley, "Come, Father, Son, and Holy Ghost," in *A Collection of Hymns for the Use of the People Called Methodists* (1780), in *A Collection of Hymns for the Use of the People Called Methodists*, ed. Franz Hildebrandt, Oliver A. Beckerlegge, and James Dale, vol. 7 of *The Works of John Wesley* (Nashville: Abingdon, 1983), 644.

27. Luke 10:35-37.

28. *The Complete Poems and Selected Letters and Prose of Hart Crane*, Bram Weber, ed. (New York: Liveright, 1988), 11.

29. See John 14:6-10.

30. See 1 John 4:11-12.

31. Written by Montesquieu about 1730, as quoted in Herbert Schlossberg, *The Silent Revolution and the Making of Victorian England* (Columbus: Ohio State University Press, 2000), 14.

32. Believe it or not, in Wesley's day the streets may have even been a bit cleaner. Jack London, *The People of the Abyss* (London: Macmillan, 1904), 78.

33. John Wesley, "To Miss March, Charlemont, June 9, 1775," in *The Letters of the Rev. John Wesley, A.M.*, ed. John Telford (London: Epworth, 1931), 6:153–54.

34. John Wesley, "On Zeal" in his *Sermons*, ed. Albert C. Outler, vol. 3 of *The Works of John Wesley* (Nashville: Abingdon, 1986), 314.

35. Matthew 5:43-48.

36. Quoted in Harold Begbie, *The Life of General William Booth: The Founder of the Salvation Army* (New York: Macmillan, 1920), 2:429.

4. The Song of Earth

1. Mark 8:18 NIV.

2. Quoted in John Winokur, ed. *Writers on Writing* (Philadelphia: Running Press, 1986), 17.

3. Walter Rauschenbusch, *Christianity and the Social Crisis* (New York: Macmillan, 1907), 420, 421.

4. For more on "What is Method acting?" see http://www.wisegeek.com/what-is-method-acting.htm.

5. The books *A Dream of Passion: The Development of the Method*, ed. Evangeline Morphos (Boston: Little, Brown, 1987; New York: New American Library, 1988), by Lee Strasberg; and *The Intent to Live: Achieving Your True Potential as an Actor* (New York: Bantam, 2005), by Larry Moss, describe not a ritualistic copy or imitation of life in Method acting but a taking on in a personal and intimate way the character to be played in order to allow that character to "live out loud" in real life.

6. Charles Wesley, "O For a Heart to Praise My God," in *A Collection of Hymns for the Use of the People Called Methodists* (1780), ed. Franz Hildebrandt, Oliver A. Beckerlegge, and James Dale, vol. 7 of *The Works of John Wesley* (Nashville: Abingdon, 1983), 491.

7. Charles Wesley, "O For a Thousand Tongues to Sing," *The United Methodist Hymnal: Book of United Methodist Worship* (Nashville: United Methodist Publishing House, 1989), 57.

8. As found in these Jewish sources: Zohar III 27b, Tikkunei Zohar 10, 13; Shir Ha-shirim Rabbah (Song of Songs) 1:11.

9. See John Wesley, "Advice to the People Called Methodists (1745)," in *The Methodist Societies: History, Nature, and Design*, ed. Rupert E. Davies, vol. 9 of *The Works of John Wesley* (Nashville: Abingdon, 1989), 123: "By Methodists I mean a people who profess to pursue . . . holiness of heart an life." See also John Wesley, "To Robert Carr Brackenbury, Bristol, September 15. 1790," in *The Letters of the Rev. John Wesley, A.M.*, ed. John Telford (London: Epworth Press, 1931), 8:238: "This doctrine is the grand depositum which God has lodged with the people called Methodists."

10. For more on the MRI operating system, see Leonard Sweet, *So Beautiful: Divine Design for Life and the Church: Missional Relational, Incarnational* (Colorado Springs, Colo.: David C. Cook, 2009).

11. See the Lay Community of St. Benedict, http://laybenedictines.org.

12. John 20:13.

13. John 1:9.

14. "I have other sheep that do not belong to this fold" (John 10:16).

15. John Donne echoed Easter when he wrote, "Death, thou shalt die." See his Holy Sonnets X, "Death, be not proud," in *The Poems of John Donne*, ed. Herbert J. C. Grierson (Oxford: Clarendon Press, 1912), 1:326.

16. See one of many posts: this one by Dwayne, age twenty-one, of Tacoma, Washington: "W/Tired Eyes, Tired Minds, Tired Souls, We Slept," posted Sept. 26, http://firstbreath90.tumblr.com/tagged/N.T._Wright.

17. John Wesley, "To John Newton," Londonderry, May 14, 1765, in Telford, *The Letters of John Wesley, A.M.*, 4:299.

18. John Wesley, "To 'John Smith'" [Sept. 28, 1745], in *Letters*, ed. Frank Baker, vol. 26 of *The Works of John Wesley* (Oxford, Clarendon Press, 1982), 2:155.

19. John Wesley, preface (1746) to *Sermons*, ed. Albert Outler, vol. 1 of *The Works of John Wesley* (Nashville: Abingdon, 1984), 1:105.

20. Russell Richey, *Early American Methodism* (Bloomington: Indiana University Press, 1991).

21. See, for example, David Brakke, *The Gnostics: Myth, Ritual, and Diversity in Early Christianity* (Cambridge, Mass.: Harvard University Press, 2010).

22. Forceyth Willson, "To Hersa," in his *Old Sergeant, and Other Poems* (Boston: Ticknor and Fields, 1867), 45. My favorite YouTube entry for this anthem, arranged by Mark Sirett, may be this one: http://www.youtube.com/watch?v=YeefxHXoNoA.

23. Warren Bennis, *On Becoming a Leader*, new and rev. ed. (Philadelphia, PA: Perseus Books, 2009), 188.

24. The phrase is that of economic historian Joel Mokyr, *The Lever of Riches: Technological Creativity and Economic Progress* (New York: Oxford University Press, 1990), 255.

25. Charles Wesley, "Hymns on the Four Gospels and Acts of the Apostles," in *The Poetical Works of John and Charles Wesley*, ed. G. Osborne, (London: Wesleyan-Methodist Conference Office, 1871), 11:334–35.

26. Ralph Waldo Emerson, entry for May 25, 1843, in *The Journals of Ralph Waldo Emerson 1820–1872*, ed. Edward Waldo Emerson and Waldo Emerson Forbes (Boston: Houghton Mifflin, 1911), 6:410.

27. See 1 Corinthians 13, but the quote is from William Shakespeare, *Macbeth*, act 5, scene 5.

28. B. Flanagan, "Johnny Cash, American," *Musician* (May 1988): 111.

29. David Benham, *Memoirs of James Hutton, Comprising the Annals of His Life and Connections with the United Brethren* (London: Hamilton, Adams, 1856), 47.

30. Gareth Lloyd, "'Running After Strange Women': An Insight into John Wesley's Troubled Marriage from a Newly Discovered Manuscript Written by His Wife," *Proceedings of the Wesley Historical Society* 53 (May 2002): 169–74.

31. Richard Challoner, *A Caveat Against the Methodists: Shewing How Unsafe It Is for Any Christian to Join Himself to Their Society, or to Adhere to Their Teachers: To Which Is Added the Catholic Devotion to the Blessed Virgin Mary*, 3d ed. (London: Printed by J. P. Coghlan, near Grosvenor-Square, 1787). This roused Wesley's Protestant wrath, and he replied in terms very different from those of his remarkably irenic "Letter to a Roman Catholic" written at Dublin in 1749.

32. Roger Kamien, *Music: An Appreciation*, 8th ed. (Boston: McGraw-Hill Higher Education, 2004), 39.

33. Charles Simeon, *Memoirs of the Life of the Rev. Charles Simeon, with a Selection from His Writings and Correspondence*, ed. William Carus; American ed., ed. Chas. P. McIlvaine (New York: Robert Carter, 1847), 105–106n.

34. John Wesley, [Monday, December 20, 1784], in *Journals*, ed. W. Reginald Ward and Richard Heitzenrater, vol. 23 of *The Works of John Wesley* (Nashville: Abingdon, 1995), 6:339.

35. John Wesley, "Catholic Spirit," in Outler, *Sermons*, 2:90. The quote within the quote is from 2 Kings 10:15, the text of the sermon.

36. John Wesley, as quoted in David Hempton, *Methodism: Empire of the Spirit* (New Haven, CT: Yale University Press, 2005), 42.

37. Edward St. Aubyn, *At Last* (London: Picador, 2011), 42.

38. Robin Hood's Bay, Wednesday, June 24, 1761: "In the midst of the sermon a large cat, frighted out of a chamber, leaped down upon a woman's head and ran over the heads or shoulders of many more. But none of them moved or cried out, any more than if it had been a butterfly." Ward and Heitzenrater, *Journals and Diaries*, 4:332.

39. John 13:35.

40. Charles Wesley, "Jesus, United by Thy Grace," *A Collection of Hymns for the Use of the People Called Methodists* (1780), in *A Collection of Hymns* (Nashville: Abingdon, 1983), 678.

41. 1 John 4:12.

42. Ephesians 4:13.

43. Thomas Aquinas makes this argument most forcefully. See, for example, his *Summa Theologiae: The Grace of Christ*, trans. Liam G. Walsh, Summa Theologiae 49 (3a.7-15) (New York: Cambridge University Press, 2006), 22 [Latin]; 23 [English].

44. 1 Corinthians 13:13.

45. John Reynolds, ed., *Anecdotes of the Rev. John Wesley* (Leeds: H. Cullingworth, 1828), 9.

46. Hebrews 11:6.

47. 1 John 5:4 NIV.

48. Iris Murdoch, "Vision and Choice in Morality," in her *Existentialists and Mystics: Writings on Philosophy and Literature* (New York: Allen Lane, 1998), 84.

49. John Wesley, "The Nature Design and General Rules of the United Societies," in Davies, *The Methodist Societies*: "*First*, By doing no harm, by avoiding evil in every kind" (70). "*Secondly*, By doing good, by being in every kind merciful after their power, as they have opportunity doing good of every possible sort and as far as possible to all men" (71). "*Thirdly*, By attending upon all the ordinances of God" (72).

50. Mark 12:30.

51. All or parts of these phrases appear in a number of John Wesley's sermons. See, for example, "The Important Question," in Outler, *Sermons*, 3:91.

52. John Wesley, "To Alexander Mather [Bristol, August 6,] 1777," in Telford, *The Letters of the Rev. John Wesley*, 6:272.

Interactives

1. Mother Teresa, *In the Silence: Meditations*, comp. Kathryn Spink (London: SPCK, 1983), 19–20.

2. Henrik Ibsen, *Brand: A Dramatic Poem in Five Acts*, trans. C. H. Herford (London: Heinemann, 1984), 2.

3. Conrad H. Gempf, *Jesus Asked: What He Wanted to Know* (Grand Rapids, Mich.: Zondervan, 2003), 28–32.

4. Arnold S. Oh, "Missions: Letting the Gospel Translate Us," in *Generation Rising: A Future with Hope for The United Methodist Church*, ed. Andrew C. Thompson (Nashville: Abingdon, 2011), 73.

5. *A Collection of Hymns for the Use of the Methodist Episcopal Church, Principally from the Collection of the Rev. John Wesley*, rev. and corrected, with a Supplement (New York: G. Lane and C. B. Tippett, 1845), 218–19.

6. Garret Keizer, *The Unwanted Sound of Everything We Want: A Book About Noise* (New York: Public Affairs, 2010), 71n, 126–127, 269, 127.